FROM DIGITAL DIVIDE
TO DIGITAL DEMOCRACY

Eleanor,
Para mi
querida amiga,
Alfredo

Edited by

Gerardo E. de los Santos
Alfredo G. de los Santos Jr.
Mark David Milliron

Dear Eleanor,
With warm wishes,
Gerardo E. de los Santos

Eleanor,
Best wishes from
all at the League!
Mark Milliron

League for Innovation in the Community College

The League for Innovation in the Community College is an international organization dedicated to catalyzing the community college movement. The League hosts conferences and institutes, develops Web resources, conducts research, produces publications, provides services, and leads projects and initiatives with more than 750 member colleges, 100 corporate partners, and a host of other government and nonprofit agencies in a continuing effort to make a positive difference for students and communities. Information about the League and its activities is available at www.league.org.

Requests for permission should be sent to
League for Innovation in the Community College
4505 E. Chandler Boulevard, Suite 250
Phoenix, AZ 85048
e-mail: publications@league.org
fax: (480) 705-8201

Printed in the United States of America.
ISBN 1-931300-36-4

TABLE OF CONTENTS

ACKNOWLEDGMENTS

This book is the work of many dedicated educators and colleagues who are committed to providing educational opportunities and information access for all students. *Mil gracias* (a thousand thanks) to the contributing authors who selflessly shared their Digital Democracy experiences and successes in the chapters that follow. Without their generous contributions, this book would not have been possible.

Special thanks to Amado M. Peña, Jr., internationally renowned Southwestern artist and Laredo Community College Distinguished Graduate, for creating and donating the cover art for this book. Peña's commitment to and support of community colleges is highly regarded, and we are delighted and honored that he is partnering with the League on this important project.

And *muchismas gracias* (very special thanks) to our colleagues at the League who reviewed the manuscript, Boo Browning and Cynthia Wilson. At the League, we proudly tout that our accomplishments are team efforts; the reviewing of this book was clearly such an achievement. To that end, we also acknowledge and thank the League support staff who daily assist our efforts to ensure quality in everything we do.

TOWARD A SHIFT IN DISCOURSE

Gerardo E. de los Santos, Alfredo G. de los Santos Jr.,
and Mark David Milliron

Community colleges continue to play a critical role in helping address societal technology access and learning needs. But our work rests in the context of the recent national discourse on the Digital Divide, which includes the often conflicting perspectives of IT access and literacy needs held by government officials, policymakers, and educators. This book, *From Digital Divide to Digital Democracy,* describes the changing nature of the Digital Divide conversation, particularly in the community college sector, from explorations and arguments about haves and have-nots to deeper, more varied dialogues about living well in an increasingly technology-enabled and connected world.

The publication is one of many League efforts aimed at inspiring community college educators to champion information technology access and instruction for a growing number of underserved and economically challenged populations. In this book, we once again engage community college educators to share with us their research, strategies, and model programs around technology access and instruction, to give readers a flavor of what the major issues are and what shape possible solutions might take.

This publication, however, marks a clear shift from the preliminary discourse about hardware, software, and Internet access issues to more in-depth and diverse explorations from multiple perspectives. Specifically, we designed the publication to explore technology access and literacy from the perspective of (1) urban community colleges, (2) rural community colleges, (3) suburban community colleges, (4) tribal colleges, (5) African-American students, (6) Hispanic students, and (7) female students. Of course there are many other angles we could have taken; nonetheless, these perspectives shed considerable light on emerging issues and helped us take the next step in our equity, diversity, and technology initiatives.

To give a better idea of these perspectives and the associated issues and insights, we will describe the chapters below. We will close here with our thoughts about why now is the time to make the shift in our conversations about these issues–a shift from championing solutions to the Digital Divide to embracing solutions for a Digital Democracy. These ideas are more fully explored in the final chapter, "On the Road to DotCalm in Education."

Chapters, Issues, and Insights

The issues, insights, model programs, successful strategies, and research outcomes shared with us by our contributing authors show how some of the most innovative community colleges are continuing to support the forward progress leading our students and communities from Digital Divide to Digital Democracy.

The Digital Divide Redefined: Some Progress Made, But the Gap Remains. Multiple sources from various segments of society, education, business, and government show that progress has been made to narrow the gap between those who have access to information technology and those who do not have access. Yet the data clearly reveal the Divide continues to exist between the IT haves and have-nots. Indeed, in some cases the Divide is growing, and the current state of IT access across income, racial and ethnic group, household, education, gender, and age still makes it quite difficult to argue that we are a nation online.

The Community College: On-Ramp to the Cyberhighway. This chapter highlights The Community College of Baltimore County's (CCBC) outreach, partnerships, and campus-based efforts to successfully serve a large number of lower-income and minority students and provide an underserved, urban community with access to the information highway. Specifically, authors describe CCBC's two-pronged approach to address the Digital Divide by focusing first on the needs of urban students enrolled at the college and then on the needs of the broader urban community.

Subdivisions: The Digital Divide in Suburban Communities.
After extensive research conducted at Sinclair Community College and
Johnson County Community College, the authors of this chapter believe
there is serious reason to explore the gaps in access and use of technology
within suburban communities. They describe several Digital Divides
occurring among groups within suburban community college areas:
(1) age-based and generation-based Digital Divides, (2) social-culture
divides, (3) divides within the ranks of the affluent, i.e., those who dislike
technology and those who embrace it, (4) divides between faculty and
younger students, and (5) divides along gender lines.

Rural Community Colleges and the Digital Divide. Rural
community colleges grapple with particular Digital-Divide issues based
on multiple challenges including remoteness, poor funding, small
populations, and relatively fewer local business partnership opportunities.
This chapter further describes the access challenges that rural colleges
face, and provides creative strategies for overcoming these obstacles.

Hispanics, the Digital Divide, and Community Colleges. Data from
Census 2000 indicate that Hispanics are the fastest growing ethnic group
in the United States. Given community colleges' long history of serving
this cohort, it is not surprising that large numbers of Hispanics are
knocking at our open door. This chapter further examines Hispanic
demographics, as well as the Digital Democracy strategies and programs
of two community colleges, Laredo Community College (TX) and Santa
Ana College (CA), that primarily serve Hispanic students and
communities.

**We Have the Hook-Up: Developing Effective Technology
Programs for the African-American Community.** This chapter focuses
on the implications of the Digital Divide as they relate to African
Americans nationwide and specifically to African Americans in the St.
Louis Community College area. From computer education in Welfare-to-
Work training programs, to IT training at community institutions, to
family computer ownership programs, to partnering with Cisco in
providing network training in low-income St. Louis neighborhoods, this
chapter describes how St. Louis Community College is committed to
supporting creative solutions that further Digital Democracy.

Technological Innovation via Education: Some Guidelines for Building Partnerships with Tribal Communities. Technology is often heralded as the solution to many of the challenges facing underserved populations. Unfortunately, without effective strategies and committed leadership, technology solutions often fail underserved populations. This chapter describes how the Tulalip Tribes looked toward the educational community for technical guidance and educational support to integrate information systems that serve all tribal members and employees, as well as provide access to services and data important to external communities. Specifically, this chapter describes the development of a Digital Divide partnership between the Tulalip Tribes, Everett Community College, and the University of Washington, Bothell, a partnership that is building a vision of the future for the Tulalip Tribes while preserving their culture.

Tunneling Through the Cyberpipes: Women in Technology in the Community College. While women outnumber men on community college campuses, barriers associated with the Digital Divide as well as to participation in math, science, and engineering fields continue to impede women in higher education, business, and the home. This chapter shares the results of a study of women in academic technology leadership roles, exploring gender issues, access, and use of information technology.

On the Road to DotCalm in Education. As we recover from the irrational-exuberance-filled dotcom journey of the last seven years, this chapter shares the perspectives of thoughtful educators who argue that we need to slow down, look around, and head down the road to DotCalm–a place where we can flesh out the good, bad, and ugly of technology in education while focusing first on the people and passions that make learning and life important. As we take this journey, however, we'll need to be on the lookout for significant individual, organizational, and societal hazards we'll encounter on the road ahead.

Why the Shift to a Dialogue on Digital Democracy

The trendy term Digital Divide has certainly led to heated debate during the last 10 years. The debate grew even hotter as our societal adoption of technology reached unprecedented levels, and many communities looked on as this digital world passed them by. Clearly, the Digital Divide should not surprise us; it is merely the technological manifestation of divides that have long existed in our society. And although debating the actual existence of a divide has become full-time work for some, we prefer to shift the debate and engage a different dialogue.

Exploring the work in this book, we see clearly that the community college is once again living and serving in its role as democracy's college. And given that we are obviously living in a Digital Democracy–a society increasingly connected, persuaded, and tracked by technology while still emphasizing individual freedom of choice–it is all the more imperative that we in community colleges embrace our traditionally inclusive role. We must engage our students not only in learning about and with technology, but also in reaching beyond technology. To serve our students well, we must be not only diligent about weaving technology into learning, but also determined about weaving learning into technology.

This bold and colorful new tapestry needs a strand of caution, too. As in any inclusive system, a Digital Democracy invites certain risks. We must equip our students with the information and ability to perceive the dangers of a digital planet along with its many marvels. In a world where marketers can analyze our every shopping habit, hate groups can manipulate and connect online with the loneliest of souls, terrorist groups can leverage technology to recruit and spread their evil, and political forces can use e-tools to target messages as never before, our students need our help. They need our help not only to earn well, but also to learn well, so they can live well. Our students need to learn not only how to use technology, but also how not to be used by it or through it. Their ability to live free in a Digital Democracy lies in the balance.

CHAPTER 1

THE DIGITAL DIVIDE REDEFINED: SOME PROGRESS MADE, BUT THE GAP REMAINS

Alfredo G. de los Santos Jr.

In a society whose economy is increasingly based on the use of the Internet, access to and use of information technologies are imperative. Those individuals and families who do not have high-speed access to the Internet will not only be at a significant disadvantage, but also will not contribute to the economic development and well-being of their country, which must compete in a global economy. In such a competitive worldwide atmosphere, the United States needs all its citizens to be part of a technology-savvy workforce.

The federal government has generally used two measures of access to information technologies: the number of households with computers at home and the share of homes with access to the Internet. These two metrics have been used in other countries including Australia, Canada, Italy, Japan, and Sweden.

In the League's *Access in the Information Age: Community Colleges Bridging the Digital Divide,* information from the Falling Through the Net series published by the National Telecommunications and Information Administration (NTIA) was used to define the Digital Divide by these two measures. Progress made using these standards will be examined here in some detail. This chapter will also include other facets, such as access to high-speed services and computer and online access by individuals.

The data in *Toward Digital Inclusion,* the latest report of the NTIA series, show that a gap remained and in some instances increased, and that the income, education, race or ethnicity, age, geography, and type of household are important determinants.

American Households With a Computer

Significant numbers of Americans bought home computers between December 1998 and August 2000. The percentage of American households with computers jumped from 42.1 percent to 51 percent; by August 2000, 53.7 million households had a computer (NTIA, 2000, p. 2).

Households in rural areas also made impressive gains, almost reaching parity with all American households. Almost half (49.6 percent) of all rural families had a computer at home by August 2000, compared with less than 40 percent only 20 months prior, in 1998.

By Income

Whether families lived in rural, urban, or center-city areas, more than 86 percent of those with incomes of $75,000 or more had a computer at home. Less than one-third (31.4 percent) of families whose annual income was between $20,000 and $24,999 owned computers. Approximately one in five families with incomes between $10,000 and $14,999 owned a computer (NTIA, 2000, p. 95).

By Race/Ethnic Group

The divide between White households and both African-American and Hispanic households continues, notwithstanding the fact that some progress was made by both of the latter groups between December 1998 and August 2000.

The number of both African-American and Hispanic households with computers at home increased from approximately one-quarter in 1998 to approximately one-third in 2000–32.6 percent and 33.7 percent, respectively.

During this same period, the number of White households with a computer increased from 46.6 percent to 55.7 percent, and almost two-thirds of Asian Americans and Pacific Islanders had computers.

The gap between Whites and African Americans continued at approximately 23 percentage points, and the divide between White and Hispanic households continued to be about 22 percentage points (NTIA, 2000, p. 16).

Large gaps remain between the shares of African-American and Hispanic households with a computer, but the gaps seem to be stabilized; at least, they did not widen from 1998 to 2000 (NTIA, 2000, p. 17).

By Race/Ethnic Group and Income

The combined factors of racial/ethnic group membership and income have been defining points in the Digital Divide. In August 2000, approximately 12 percent of African-American and Hispanic households with incomes of less than $15,000 a year had computers, compared with 87 percent of White households with incomes of more than $75,000 (NTIA, 2000, p. 96).

By Educational Level

The link between level of education and household ownership of a computer continued to be as significant in 2000 as it was in 1998. More than three-quarters of all households with members holding a bachelor's degree or higher had a computer in 2000, whether in rural or urban areas; in the central city, 72.2 percent of those with a bachelor's or higher had computers.

About one in five families (21.9 percent) with some high school education owned a computer, compared with approximately two in five (39.6 percent) whose members had a high school diploma or GED. More than 60 percent of households whose members reported some college education owned a computer.

One in five rural households with some high school education had a computer at home, compared with three-quarters of all families with a bachelor's degree.

By Household Type

Households made up of a married couple with children younger than 18 were twice as likely to have a computer (60.6 percent) as female-headed households with children under 18 (30 percent).

Approximately 30 percent of nonfamily households and 35 percent of households headed by males with no children owned computers. Two in five family households without children under 18 had a computer at home.

Households With Internet Access

In the 20-month period from December 1998 to August 2000, the percentage of households with access to the Internet grew from 26.2 percent to 41.5 percent, an increase of almost 60 percent. Thus, more than 80 percent of all households with computers have Internet access.

Almost all groups made progress in Internet access; however, the gap between groups continued and in some instances actually increased. The determinants of whether a household has access to the Internet are the same factors that influence whether a household has a computer at home.

By Income

A strong connection exists between household income and access to the Internet. More than three-quarters (77.7 percent) of all families with annual income of $75,000 or more had access to the Internet in August 2000, compared with 60.3 percent in 1998.

Approximately one-third (34 percent) of households with incomes between $25,000 and $34,999 had Internet access, while only 12.7 percent of households with incomes of less than $15,000 did (NTIA, 2000, p. 8).

By Race/Ethnicity

While 41.5 percent of American households had Internet access in August 2000, households of Asian Americans and Pacific Islanders had the highest Internet penetration at 56.8 percent. White households had the second highest at 46.1 percent.

African-American households almost doubled in terms of access to the Internet, from 11.2 percent in 1998 to 23.5 percent in August 2000. Access among Hispanic households increased significantly in the 20-month period, from 12.5 percent to 23.6 percent (NTIA, 2000, p. 13).

Nevertheless, the gap between both African-American and Hispanic households and the national average has actually increased. The Internet-access divide between the number of African-American households and the national average was three percentage points larger in 2000 than the gap that existed in 1998–15 percentage points in 1998 compared with 18 percentage points, representing a 23.5 percent penetration rate for African-American households, compared with 41.5 percent for all households.

The access gap for Hispanic households increased from 13.6 percentage points in 1998 to 17.9 percentage points in 2000, an increase of 4.3 points–a 23.6 percent rate for Hispanic households, compared with 41.5 percent for households nationally (NTIA, 2000, pp. 13, 16).

By Race/Ethnicity and Income

By August of 2000, more than three-quarters of all households with incomes of $75,000 or more had access to the Internet, compared with 60.3 percent in 1998. Of households with incomes of $75,000 or more, 63.7 percent of Hispanic, 81.5 percent of Asian-American and Pacific-Islander, 70.9 percent of African-American, and 78.6 percent of White households had Internet access.

But income seems to be as important a determinant of the Digital Divide as race or ethnicity. Almost four of five White households with incomes of $75,000 or more had Internet access, while only 5.2 percent of Hispanic families and 6.4 percent of African-American families with incomes of less than $15,000 did (NTIA, 2000, p. 99).

By Education

Rates of households with access to the Internet increased markedly for all educational levels in the 20-month period from December 1998 to August 2000. A strong relationship persists between education and Internet access.

Almost 70 percent of all households with a postgraduate degree had access to the Internet in August 2000, compared with almost 30 percent of households with high school graduates. Slightly more than one in 10 households with less than a high school education (11.7 percent) had Internet access, though the rate for this group more than doubled in the 20-month period.

By Household Type

Six out of 10 households made up of married couples with children younger than 18 had access to the Internet in August 2000. About one-third of male households with children under 18, and only three of 10 households led by women with children younger than 18 had Internet access. Female households with children under 18 in urban and central-city areas had the least access–29.7 and 22.8 percent, respectively (NTIA, 2000, p. 100).

By Age

In August 2000, more than half of all American households in two age groups had access to the Internet: 52.3 percent in the 34-to-44 age group and 51.9 percent in the group aged 45 to 54. Only one-third of households fitting these categories had access in 1998.

About one in four (26 percent) of all householders older than 55 had Internet access. More than one-third (35.7 percent) of all householders under 25 years of age had access (NTIA, 2000, p. 100).

High-Speed Internet Access

As the country's technology infrastructure evolves, an important change has been the development of faster transmission speeds and wider bandwidth. In effect, broadband higher-speed access services were used by only 10.7 percent of those households with access to the Internet in August 2000. Though that figure represents only 4.5 percent of all American households, it is an important development.

Of those households that did have broadband access in August 2000, approximately half (50.8 percent) used cable modems and about one-third (33.7 percent) used Digital Subscriber Line (DSL). The rest used wireless, satellite, and other telephone-based technologies.

Broadband penetration by geography varies, with the highest (12.2 percent) in the central cities and the lowest (7.3 percent) in rural areas. A relationship exists between household income and use of broadband services: the most affluent households, with incomes of $75,000 or more, have double the penetration of low-income households.

Use of the faster transmission service seems to be inversely related to age. Younger households have the highest broadband penetration (12.3 percent). Hispanic (8.9 percent) and African-American (9.8 percent) households rank somewhat below both Asian-American/Pacific-Islander (11.7 percent) and White households (10.8 percent).

Access to high-speed transmission services will become more and more important in the future, as the technological infrastructure grows and develops. The divide, even at this early stage of evolution, is obvious (NTIA, 2000, pp. 23-24).

Internet Use by Individuals

According to the NTIA report, more than 116 million individual Americans–or 44.4 percent of the total population 3 years of age and older–used the Internet as of August 2000. That is almost 32 million more than in December 1998.

By Income

The higher the household income, the higher the individual use rate of the Internet. Seven out of 10 individuals in households with incomes of more than $75,000 use the Internet. A little over one-third (35.7 percent) of the individuals in households with incomes between $25,000 and $34,999 use the Internet. Fewer than one in five (18.9 percent) of individuals in households with less than $15,000 annual income use the Internet (NTIA, 2000, pp. 36-37).

By Race/Ethnicity

While use of the Internet is increasing, as noted above, use varies by different racial/ethnic groups. The gap between groups increased from 1998 to 2000.

Approximately half of Whites (50.3 percent) and Asian-Americans/Pacific Islanders (49.4 percent) were using the Internet in August 2000. Almost one in three (29.3 percent) African Americans used the Internet in 2000, compared with less than one in four (19 percent) in 1998. In 2000, less than one-quarter (23.7 percent) of Hispanics used the Internet, compared with 16.6 percent in 1998.

Though the percentage of African-American and Hispanic individuals who use the Internet increased, the gap between these two groups and Whites increased as well. While African Americans were 18.6 percentage points behind Whites in 1998, by 2000, the difference was 21.3–an increase of 2.7 percentage points in the divide.

In 1998, the gap between Whites and Hispanics was 21 percentage points; by August 2000, the gap had increased by 5.6 percentage points, to 26.6 percent (NTIA, 2000, pp. 37-38).

By Gender

By August 2000, 44.6 percent of men and 44.2 percent of women were using the Internet. In the early years, both boys and girls used the

Internet at the same rate. A higher percentage of women than men in the 18-to-45 age group use the Internet. More men than women older than 50 use the Internet, but the rate of use declines with age (NTIA, 2000, p. 39).

By Gender and Race/Ethnicity

In August 2000, women and men in all racial and ethnic groups, with the exception of Asian Americans and Pacific Islanders, had very similar Internet-use rates. Among that exception group, more men than women used the Internet (NTIA, 2000, pp. 39-40).

By Education

Almost three-quarters (74.5 percent) of individuals who had earned a bachelor's degree or higher were using the Internet, compared with three out of 10 (30.6 percent) whose greatest level of educational attainment was high school.

More than half (54.2 percent) of those who had some college education used the Internet, while only 12.7 percent of those who were not high school graduates used it (NTIA, 2000, pp. 40-41).

By Age

Individuals were grouped into different age categories: 3 to 8; 9 to 17; 18 to 24; 25 to 49; and 50 and above. All age groups had increases in the use of the Internet from 1998 to 2000, but there are gaps among racial/ethnic categories within some of the age groups. The children in the 3-to-8 age group had the lowest rate of Internet use: 15.3 percent (NTIA, 2000, p. 41).

Age 9 to 17

More than half (53.4 percent) of all individuals in this age group used the Internet by August 2000. There was little difference between boys (52.9 percent) and girls (53.9 percent) in use of the Internet in this age group.

The divide in Internet use by individuals from racial/ethnic groups was marked, with Whites (63.1 percent) and Asian Americans/Pacific Islanders (58.6 percent) showing larger use rates than did African Americans, at 34.2 percent, and Hispanics, at 31.4 percent (NTIA, 2000, p. 42).

Age 18 to 24

In this age group, 56.8 percent of all individuals used the Internet. Women (59.6 percent) had a higher rate of Internet use than did men (54.1 percent).

Asian Americans and Pacific Islanders had the highest rate of Internet use (72.9 percent), followed by Whites (65 percent). Approximately one in four (41.5 percent) African Americans and almost one-third (32.4 percent) of Hispanics used the Internet (NTIA, 2000, p. 42).

Age 25 to 49

Labor-force status seems to be an important determinant of the use of the Internet for individuals in this age group. The overall Internet use rate for all individuals in this age group was 55.4 percent in August 2000. However, almost six out of 10 (58.4 percent) of those in the labor force used the Internet, compared with less than four out of 10 (39.3 percent) of those who were not in the labor force.

Six of 10 women in this age bracket who were in the labor force used the Internet, compared with 56.2 percent of the men. The Internet use rate for women not in the labor force was higher than the use rate for men: 42.5 percent and 28.6 percent, respectively.

The rate of Internet use by African Americans and Hispanics was below the national average, but those who were not in the labor force were even further below the average numbers. For African Americans in the labor force, the rate of Internet use was 40.3 percent, but for those not in the labor force, it was 18.9 percent.

The Internet use rate for Hispanics in the labor force was 29.8 percent; the rate for those outside the labor force was only 16.5 percent (NTIA, 2000, p. 44).

Age 50 and Over

Fewer than one in three (29.6 percent) of individuals 50 years of age or older used the Internet in August 2000. Almost half (46.4 percent) of those in the labor force used the Internet, but only 16.6 percent of those not in the labor force used it–a three-to-one ratio (NTIA, 2000, p. 45).

Participation in the labor force affects the gender difference for individuals in this age category. The use rate of both men and women who were still in the labor force in August 2000 was about the same–46 percent for men and 46.8 percent for women.

However, only 15.6 percent of the women not in the labor force used the Internet, compared with 18.1 percent of the men who were not in the labor force.

Conclusion

In the 20-month period from December 1998 to August 2000, the data indicate that significant progress has been made in both ownership of computers and in access to the Internet by an increasing number of American households. More than half of all American households had a computer at home, and four out of 10 households had access to the Internet.

However, the NTIA in *Toward Digital Inclusion* reports that "a Digital Divide remains or has expanded slightly in some cases, even with Internet access and computer ownership rising rapidly for almost all groups. For example, our most recent data show that divides still exist between those with different levels of income and education, between different racial and ethnic groups, old and young, single- and dual-parent families, and those with and without disabilities" (NTIA, 2000, p. xvi).

The profile of the have-nots continues to be very similar to that of the students served by the community colleges in this country, as reported in the League's *Access in the Information Age.*

Increases in computer ownership and in access to the Internet are "occurring among most groups of Americans, regardless of income, education, race or ethnicity, location, age, or gender, *suggesting that digital inclusion is a realizable goal*" (emphasis added) (NTIA, 2000, p. xv).

Community colleges will continue to play an increasingly important part in bridging the Digital Divide.

REFERENCE

National Telecommunications and Information Administration. (2000). *Falling Through the Net: Toward Digital Inclusion.* Washington, DC: NTIA, U.S. Department of Commerce. www.ntia.doc.gov/ntiahome/ digitaldivide/.

Chapter 2

The Community College: On-Ramp to the Cyberhighway

Edward Leach and Irving Pressley McPhail

More and more Americans are using information technology, going online to conduct business, communicate, find information, and take classes. With each passing year, as information technology and the Internet become increasingly more important to the nation's economy, communities that lack access to computers and Web-based resources are at a distinct and growing disadvantage. Inadequate access to information technology or the equipment necessary to gain entry onto the information highway is resulting in a greater disparity between those with access and those without.

Those communities without access to information technology and less able to travel the information highway risk getting left in the dust. Only with access to technology and Web-based resources will communities be adequately prepared for the jobs of the future, as well as the advantages provided by the services and information that continue moving to the Internet.

Ownership Access in Minority, Urban, and Low-Income Households

The fourth report of the *Falling Through the Net* series, *Toward Digital Inclusion* (2000), examined the number of households and individuals who have computers and access to the Internet for the period December 1998 to August 2000. The findings show that access to computers and to the Internet is rapidly increasing, with the overall number of households with computers up to 51 percent, from 42.1 percent, and those with Internet access rising from 26.2 percent to 41.5 percent.

However, African Americans and Hispanics still lag behind other groups, and the computer gap between high- and low-income Americans is large and growing. While 93 percent of households earning more than $75,000 per year own computers, only 40 percent of households earning less than $30,000 per year own them. Households earning more than $75,000 are consistently likely to own computers (87 percent for White households, 83.4 percent for African Americans, and 76.1 percent for Hispanics). At incomes less than $15,000, African-American households (11.5 percent) and Hispanic households (12.5 percent) are less likely to have computers than White households (22.8 percent).

Households in central cities had much lower rates of increase in Internet penetration than other areas. In August 2000, 3.8 percent fewer central-city households had Internet access, compared with the national average. In December 1998, the percentage of central-city households was 1.7 percent lower than the national rate, indicating that the gap appears to be growing rather than narrowing in terms of household access to the Internet in central cities. African-American households in central cities registered an access rate slightly below the national average for African Americans. Hispanic households in central cities also had an access rate slightly below the national average for Hispanic households. White central-city households had an Internet access rate up from December 1998. Urban households with incomes of $75,000 or higher are over 20 times more likely to have access to the Internet than rural households at the lowest income levels, and more than nine times more likely to have a computer at home.

The New Economy Workforce and Community College Students

The transformation of our society to a knowledge-based economy has increased the demand for highly skilled information technology workers in manufacturing, transportation, health care, education, and government. In spite of the dotcom fallout and the recent slowdown in the economy, the IT field remains the fastest-growing economy around the globe. The Information Technology Association of America (ITAA) points out that the IT industry workforce consists of 10.4 million individuals, but needs to grow between 7 and 10 percent annually to keep pace with worldwide demand.

But it appears that the number of IT workers being prepared for the workforce is falling short of the number of workers needed. The Bureau of Labor Statistics (BLS) forecasts that employment in the IT service segment of the industry alone will need to double by the year 2005, yet the ITAA warns that 425,000 jobs requiring information technology skills in 2001 went unfilled because of a shortage of qualified workers. The difficulty of preparing IT workers fast enough to meet workforce needs appears not to be an issue of undesirable salaries limiting new entries into the profession. Individuals with the requisite IT skills are receiving fast-rising salaries and salaries that are higher than those of other workers.

Although many IT workers get their formal training for high-paying technology-related positions at four-year institutions, community colleges are frequently becoming the training ground for IT workers. With certificate programs increasingly becoming the rite of entry into IT jobs, many students are choosing to begin their technical education in certificate programs found on community college campuses.

In spite of the high number of minorities attending our nation's community colleges, generally, minorities are considerably underrepresented in community college IT programs and in the IT workforce. And the shortage of minorities in the IT workforce is largely due to their underrepresentation in the technical education pipeline that leads to these jobs. Because nearly 50 percent of minority college students start their education at a community college (Foote, 1997), these institutions are well positioned for establishing strategies to recruit and retain talented minority students in IT programs.

A Call to Action

In their 2001 work, *Access in the Information Age: Community Colleges Bridging the Digital Divide*, de los Santos, de los Santos Jr., and Milliron recognize that America's community colleges are well positioned to assist in bridging the Digital Divide; they rightfully call on community colleges to "move beyond definition and dialogue about the Digital Divide and take action" (p. 10). The authors' identification of community colleges as the ideal institutions for closing the gap between the technology haves and have-nots stems in part from the fact that, although community colleges are well known for serving students wishing to obtain an associate degree or transfer to baccalaureate institutions, many community colleges also have developed innovative programs and projects designed to keep students up to date on the latest developments in technology-related equipment, software, and skills.

Another factor that makes community colleges the ideal organizations to tackle the Digital Divide is that nearly half of all minorities enrolled in higher education attend two-year colleges. Likewise, community colleges tend to enroll more students who do not own their own computers; while 58 percent of all postsecondary students own computers, only 40 percent of those students attending public two-year institutions own computers (Web-Based Education Commission, 2000).

Community colleges have a rich history of collaboration with other organizations within their communities. Community colleges work closely with the private sector, community-based organizations, and other educational institutions to serve their local communities, a characteristic that can prove valuable given the high cost of providing technology-related equipment and training. Community-based partnerships that bring together local organizations have proved effective in providing underserved communities with access to technology at considerably lower cost than when individual organizations try bridging the Digital Divide on their own (Johnson, et al., 2000).

Finally, almost every community college must, as part of its mission, serve the specific needs of its local community. By providing minority and lower-income communities access to the technology and Web-based resources to which they otherwise might not have access, community colleges fulfill their acknowledged mission to serve the local community and its students.

The League for Innovation, through its Digital Divide efforts, is challenging community colleges to work with their local private sector and community-based organizations and other educational institutions to provide access to technology and Web-based resources for minority and lower-income communities. In responding to the League's challenge, community colleges have developed a variety of strategies to help provide individuals with access to computers, the Internet, and Web-based resources that prepare students for the jobs of today and of the future. Of particular interest are the efforts of urban community colleges that serve large populations of minority and lower-income communities, because even as more and more Americans connect to the Internet from their homes, data show that libraries and schools, including community colleges, are critical to urban citizens who do not have this access at home.

It is abundantly clear that without the efforts of urban community colleges, individuals within these communities will have fewer opportunities in the Digital Age. This chapter highlights one urban community college's outreach, partnerships, and campus-based efforts to successfully serve a large number of lower-income and minority students, and to provide an underserved community with access to the information highway.

The Community College of Baltimore County: An Urban Community College

Urban community colleges play a critical role in higher education by serving large educationally disadvantaged student populations often consisting of low-income, first-generation, minority students. These urban institutions are critical to the nation's future, as they provide opportunities for individuals who would most likely lack other access to higher education and the technology that can prepare them to enter the information technology workforce. The Community College of Baltimore County (CCBC), formed in 1998 as a result of a merger of three colleges in Baltimore County, is an institution that serves a growing low-income, minority, and urban community.

Addressing the problem of the Digital Divide for an urban community college requires an approach integrated with the existing goals and objectives of the institution. In 1998, CCBC developed a plan, LearningFirst, based on a vision, mission, statement of beliefs, and eight strategic directions to guide CCBC to becoming a premier learning college (LearningFirst, 1998). Four of these strategic directions include operational objectives that were modified and built upon to address the specific issue of the Digital Divide. They are student learning, infusing technology, embracing diversity, and building community. CCBC has implemented a two-pronged approach to address the Digital Divide, focusing on the needs of students enrolled at the college and then on the needs of the broader community.

The first step in addressing the problem was to ascertain the degree of the Digital Divide among CCBC's students and in the Baltimore region. To do this, the college conducted a survey of its students. The results indicate that the majority of respondents (70 percent) have access to computers and the Internet–well above the average reported in national surveys. However, for many students (20 percent), primary access was through the college. For African-American students, access to computers was considerably lower, and for more of these students, primary access to computers and the Internet was at the college itself.

To determine accessibility to computers and the Internet in the broader community, the college worked with the local technology council and other groups to ascertain the need by locality and group. Again, the results were not surprising; they mirrored data from national surveys, showing that African-American neighborhoods and poorer neighborhoods had much less access to computers and the Internet.

Developing an Internal Strategy

Addressing the problem of the Digital Divide for currently enrolled students is paramount to their continued academic success. Student Learning and Infusing Technology are both strategic directions for the college, and the college chose a strategy of integrating the issue of the Digital Divide within existing college initiatives and programs as the best way to narrow the Digital Divide for students. A series of current initiatives was reviewed with an eye to reducing the gap. This strategy was determined to be the most effective, given the cost constraints faced by the college and the high cost of technology.

Unlike four-year institutions that require students to have computers, community colleges must rely on different strategies. For four-year institutions with stable populations, a computer policy based on a computer for each student makes sense. For community colleges with large part-time, poorer student populations, this approach may not be feasible. A strategy of multiple use can be much more efficient and effective.

Access and Need

CCBC is making a concerted effort to increase access to computers at its campuses. The greatest need is based on the Digital Divide survey data, as opposed to providing access strictly according to enrollment levels, as in the past. The campus with the greatest need based on the Digital Divide survey data is now given higher priority for more open-access points and more outreach efforts.

Open and Multiple-Use Computer Labs

CCBC began to increase the number of open labs for students. These open labs and homework labs were designed to provide state-of-the-art computers with Internet access, and to allow students the ability to complete computer-related work assignments on campus. The number and location of the open labs were altered in accordance with survey and demographic information to serve the most needy student populations. The operating hours for the open labs were also increased, and the college continues to look for ways to extend the hours even further.

In order to increase the number of open labs, the college has made a concerted effort to develop multiple-use labs that serve as additional open labs for students. Access is not just related to the number of computers on campus, but to the use of those computers. Labs are often dedicated to a single purpose or department, or directed to credit or continuing education only. Opening up previously dedicated labs and increasing their use requires additional personnel to staff and configure the labs, as well as resources to carefully schedule those labs.

Open Computer Stations

CCBC also began an experimental program that has proven so successful that it is being rapidly expanded. In the past two years, the college upgraded its fiber backbone and created the ability to increase the number of network drops and computer access points throughout the college. With a steady infusion of new equipment, the college faced an increasing number of older computers. Instead of surplusing this older equipment, the college placed some of these computers in student lounges and in open areas throughout the campuses. The computers include standard college software and Internet access. The implementation of these stations has been so successful that the college is expanding their use as rapidly as possible.

Student E-Mail Accounts and Web Pages

CCBC provides all its credit students with free e-mail accounts and Web pages when they enroll. Unfortunately, many students–especially those with the fewest computer skills–never take advantage of the opportunity. To get these students to seize the chance provided, the college has actively promoted the program. In addition, the college is exploring the feasibility of creating an outreach program to include continuing education students in the use of these services, particularly those students who might not have access to computers and related services at home.

Developing an External Strategy

The means to developing a successful community strategy and targeted programs is partnerships with other community and government organizations, and CCBC has developed a number of partnerships to help reduce the Digital Divide in its community. While the college's mission is focused first on students and then on the community, there are local organizations whose primary mission is community outreach. Partnering with these organizations has proven to be a successful strategy for CCBC.

Two types of partnering have taken place: direct community projects and partnerships with other organizations for broader community outreach. The college has undertaken two direct community outreach projects to date and has more in the planning stages. In both cases, the college has used surplus college computer equipment and donated equipment to complete the labs. The college has a regular computer replacement policy, and, as a result of the upgrades, has been able to provide students with surplus lower-level Pentium computers.

Turner Station Community Center

Turner Station is a historically African-American community in an economically depressed section of Baltimore County. Two years ago, the county constructed a community center complete with recreational and other facilities. The college, in conjunction with community leaders, established two 24-station computer labs at the facility. The labs were constructed in a short time using surplus college computer equipment, donated software, and volunteer labor. The college continues to maintain the labs with volunteers and additional equipment. Use of these labs by members of the community has grown steadily over time, and the college is working with the center's director to obtain direct donations of state-of-the-art equipment and Internet access for the center.

Baltimore County Detention Center

Unfortunately, large numbers of African Americans in the United States are incarcerated. In Baltimore County, individuals convicted of lesser crimes and citizens awaiting trial are housed in the county detention center. CCBC, through its outreach programs, became aware that the computer lab at the facility was not functional. The detention center lab was full of 15-year-old computers, of which only a few were even working. The college once again used surplus equipment to complete a new lab at the center. While Internet access is not allowed at the facility, inmates have made heavy use of the new lab, and classes are now being offered to help students obtain and upgrade computer skills.

While these direct projects have been successful, CCBC has also undertaken broader partnerships to increase the efficacy of its efforts in the community. The college has formed partnerships with county agencies to directly attack the problem. These partnerships include Baltimore County Public Library, Baltimore County Public Schools, and various county agencies.

Baltimore County Public Library

A central part of Baltimore County Public Library's mission is direct community outreach. CCBC has formed a strategic alliance with the library to optimize the use of resources, including the sharing of training resources. The college and the library are also undertaking the development of a new joint-use facility in a part of the county not currently served by the library or the college. To address the Digital Divide, the library has increased the number of open-access labs in poorer and African-American neighborhoods. The college is currently working with the library to broaden that access even further.

Baltimore County Public Schools

The college has had a long-term partnership with local high schools, providing service, technical support, and surplus equipment. But because of a recent infusion of newer computer equipment by the county into the schools, surplus college equipment is not needed to the degree it was in the past. Therefore, the college and the schools are looking for ways to place surplus equipment in poorer and African-American neighborhoods while also seeking ways to provide more access by the community to high school labs.

Technology Training in CCBC Programs and Courses

CCBC has addressed training and technology skills issues in a number of ways. It has increased the number and scope of its information technology classes, instituted training for its faculty to ensure they incorporate instructional technology across the curriculum, and begun setting technical-proficiency standards for its students.

To provide information technology skills and training, and to address the Digital Divide, CCBC has expanded its offerings to include providing a full array of credit and noncredit learning experiences. Through its adult education program, the college is able to offer IT training throughout the area and reach communities that might not otherwise have easy access to classes. Minority enrollments in these classes have increased dramatically. The college also has a training partnership with Baltimore County Public Library that provides free basic training in its branches for all citizens. The college and the library are looking to expand the relationship by sharing labs and expertise.

The college has also established a highly successful training program, Teachers Learning Computers in the Learning College (TLC^2). The program enables faculty to integrate instructional technology into classrooms and to use technology to provide students with alternative learning modalities. To date, most faculty have taken basic and intermediate courses, and over half have taken advanced classes. As faculty integrate technology into the classroom, more students are exposed to it and grow proficient in their computer skills.

CCBC has also come to consider the issue of technical proficiencies for all its students. It has set a technical requirement as part of its general education core and is looking to expand the issue of technical proficiency and standards.

Current Results and Future Actions

A second survey of CCBC students indicates an improvement in access to computers for students who are most at risk from the Digital Divide. More students are reporting greater access to computers and the Internet, and more of these students are reporting that the college is their primary access point to technology. Additional efforts to provide greater access to computers are in the planning stages. Among the college's future goals are selling laptops in college bookstores and getting surplus computers directly into the hands of needy students.

A final effort is being explored countywide. Given the infusion of new computer equipment at the college, local K-12 schools, and county government, these three organizations are currently exploring a partnership with a community agency that will put additional equipment in community centers in the city and county. A request for proposals is being drafted that will allow the organizations to get surplus computer equipment into the hands of those most at need on a much wider scale than ever before.

Bringing Everyone Into the Technological Mainstream

Today's students must stay current with technology in order to enter and maintain competitiveness in the job market. As technology continues to be critical to the success of the country's economy, it is in the nation's and community colleges' best interest to provide access to technology and the necessary services to students. The issue is no longer whether community colleges should be identifying strategies that help their local minority and lower-income communities gain access to technology and Web-based resources. All community colleges have a role to play, but those community colleges serving large minority and lower-income communities in the nation's urban centers have a special role in serving these communities.

This chapter presents various strategies that one urban serving community college has undertaken to prepare its community to effectively use technology as a means of becoming better prepared for the demands of the new American economy. The time has come for community colleges to take the lead in identifying strategies to help urban minority and lower-income communities access the technology and Web-based resources that will prepare them to take full advantage of the opportunities brought on by advances in the Digital Age.

Internet access is no longer a luxury item, but a resource used by many. Although computer ownership and Internet access rates are increasing for almost all groups, there are still communities that do not have adequate access to computers and technology-based training, resources, and services. Community colleges must continue to take steps to expand access to new technologies and Web-based resources until all communities have adequate access to these resources.

The League for Innovation will continue in its efforts to encourage the aggregation of resources and services to provide access to computers and technology-based training, resources, and services. Providing this access must remain a priority for community colleges, particularly those community colleges serving urban centers with high numbers of students living in minority and lower-income communities. Assisting in bridging the Digital Divide is central to the community college mission, and now is the time for these colleges to take action and "be more proactive and more aggressive in dealing with this critical social issue" (de los Santos, de los Santos Jr., & Milliron, 2001, p. 122). Collectively, community colleges represent opportunities for developing effective strategies for ensuring that all students benefit from the opportunities provided by new and emerging information technologies.

REFERENCES

de los Santos, G. E., de los Santos Jr., A. G., & Milliron, M. D. (Eds.). (2000). *Access in the Information Age: Community Colleges Bridging the Digital Divide*. Mission Viejo, CA: League for Innovation in the Community College.

Foote, E. (1997). Community Colleges: General Information and Resources. *ERIC Digest.*

Hecker, D. (June 1999). High-Technology Employment: A Broader View. *Economist, 122* (6). Washington, DC: Office of Employment Projections, Bureau of Labor Statistics.

Information Technology Association of America. (April, 2001). *When Can You Start? Building Better Information Technology Skills and Careers*. Washington, DC: Information Technology Association of America.

McPhail, I., Heacock, R., & Linck, H. (2000). LearningFirst: Creating and Leading the Learning College. *Community College Journal of Research and Practice, 25*, 17-28.

National Telecommunications and Information Administration. (2000). *Falling Through the Net: Toward Digital Inclusion*. Washington, DC: NTIA, U.S. Department of Commerce. www.ntia.doc.gov/ntiahome/ digitaldivide/.

Web-Based Education Commission. (December, 2000). *The Power of the Internet for Learning: Moving from Promise to Practice*. Washington, DC.

CHAPTER 3

SUBDIVISIONS:
THE DIGITAL DIVIDE IN SUBURBAN COMMUNITIES

Steven Lee Johnson and Douglas Allen

Are there significant gaps in access and use of technology within suburban communities? We believe there is compelling reason to explore the question.

We approached the issue of suburban Digital Divides with some initial hesitation. Why focus on the privileged when there are such obvious gaps between the haves and the have-nots? Within our respective colleges, we work to bring technology and technology training to those who live in cultures and communities historically left behind in various ways. The Digital Divide in this country has been most pronounced in the fissures occurring along important economic and racial lines (de los Santos, 2000). These major splits have captured the attention of educators as well.

Our challenge is to consider the multiple types of digital divisions within our country whose significance is not yet recognized. With clear understanding that socioeconomic and racial relationships are critical elements of the Digital Divide, we nevertheless opted to forge ahead and explore new types of technology gaps, those occurring within suburbia regardless of the assumed privileged status of suburbanites. We chose this task simply because we could not ignore the likelihood of undiscovered patterns of technology haves and have-nots within our suburban communities.

Setting aside the issue of rich versus poor, we wondered, *What if there are other significant patterns within our suburbs that, overlooked, might cause us to miss critical opportunities to fulfill our responsibility as educators?* Many of us have college service areas that span all types of communities–urban, suburban, and rural. We have a responsibility to provide education and related resources to the entire service district, regardless of differences among the communities where our college students live.

In the course of developing this chapter on suburban Digital Divides, we found virtually no literature on the subject, only comparisons of suburban technology use to urban and rural use. Working under the assumption that we are at an early stage in this particular line of research, we chose not to analyze past research findings. And even though we are working to narrow the technology gap, we resisted using this chapter to describe the best Digital Divide practices of our respective colleges.

Instead, we hope to contribute something new to the ongoing national conversation about digital divisions. Until now, all residents of suburban communities have been lumped together, considered equal, and contrasted against the economic have-nots living in the rural and urban communities. We might tend to think of those living in suburbs as setting the standard and providing social benchmarks, yet our suburban communities show gaps of their own. We propose that there are at least five important types of digital fault lines in suburban America that need and deserve further consideration to determine if they indeed exist, are valid, and are significant.

Because we had little available to us on the topic of suburban Digital Divides, our research consisted of reviewing literature and interviewing numerous college and public school officials who we thought would be able to help us begin to identify gaps in technology use and access within suburban areas. The people we talked to had a range of responsibilities and experiences that made them expert practitioners in the world of developing, maintaining, and delivering technology services to students of all ages. We interviewed professors, college department chairs, school principals, county-level education officials, computer lab technicians, teachers, and technology service managers.

Finding thoughtful and knowledgeable people who wanted to talk about the Digital Divide was fairly easy. The difficult part was keeping our focus on surfacing patterns of technology divisions within suburban communities only, instead of slipping back into comparison.

Over the course of many interviews and structured discussions, we found indications of several different types of Digital Divides occurring among groups within suburban areas. Once the issue was raised, practically all sources we talked to agreed that there are those in suburbia who have access to technology and who apply it to enrich their lives, and those who do not. Several patterns of suburban Digital Divides emerged in these interviews. In addition, and across the board, our education officials expressed a shared belief that those who do not use technology, for whatever underlying reason, are at a disadvantage compared with those who do.

The following list of Digital Divides in suburbia provides a comprehensive first attempt to define the problem. We found these possible indications of significant fractures:

- Age-based and generation-based Digital Divides
- A divide that persists between faculty and younger students who have "grown up digital" (Tapscott, 1999)
- A potentially significant divide running along gender lines
- Social culture divides along the lines of blue- and white-collar professionals
- Divides within the ranks of the affluent, i.e., those daunted by technology and those who embrace it

In the following section, we will describe the suburban Digital Divide and reasons why these categories exist. We do wish to point out that, although we present these categories as discrete entities, there is overlap and interaction among them. Distinctions are sometimes tricky to make.

Generation Gap

Several of our education practitioners contended that technology divides probably form along age lines within suburbia. The simple and generally accurate assumption is that younger people tend to take advantage of new technology; they integrate technology into their lives, and are more poised than older people to benefit from it.

A college department chair with extensive experience in developing and managing technology courses provided an interesting view of age differences in technology use among the many types of students her college serves. She described four "broad buckets" of technology savvy among the college student population:

- Younger students recently out of high school who enjoy a range of technology skills, experience, and ease
- Working professionals age 40 and younger who have ample technology skills and workplace experience, and who are comfortable with technology
- Adult re-entry students (40-60 years old) who have been homebound for several years, and who have scant technology skill or experience
- People 60 and over who have less direct experience with new technology, even when they have been employed in technology-using organizations in the past

Assuming that these four broad categories exist as described, it is important that future researchers study and understand age-related differences in technology use, for at least two reasons. The first important reason relates to meeting the educational needs of individuals in ways that are relevant to them. For now, we can assume that a group of college students just out of high school will have different technology skills and needs compared to college students in the 60-plus age group. If this assumption holds, we can argue that differing courses of study and curriculum could be designed for each group.

The second significant reason for knowing the true and accurate extent of a Digital Divide along age lines is that ultimately, we worry that our community elders might be truly disadvantaged by an age-related Digital Divide. Do working adults and very young adults have an economic or social advantage over technically less-than-tech-savvy elders?

Teachers and Students

In our interviews with educational practitioners, we asked them to think beyond the obvious in considering patterns of disparate technology use and experience. We were somewhat surprised when one of our practitioners raised the point that the most important Digital Divide may be between students and their teachers. A technological divide between students and their teachers is worrisome if students are expected to take guidance from their teachers. In subsequent interviews, several educational practitioners confirmed that more often than not, younger students are savvier and more comfortable than their teachers with basic technology.

When personal computers swept onto the stage in the early 1980s, a common sales tactic was to encourage parents to purchase computers for their children. Apple's clever commercial use of the pop lyric, "Teach your children well," rang clear for millions of suburban parents who determined not to let their children be left behind. Suburban public and private school districts closely followed these parents in adopting the technology.

While neither the parents nor the districts had clear plans about the use of these new machines, the children did have time to learn about them, play with them, and, along the way, incorporate them into their lives. School administrators and teachers were too busy with more traditional learning activities to keep up with their increasingly technology-savvy students. Consequently, the children learned the technology while educators fought for funds, experimented with substandard educational software, and generally did a second-drawer job of integrating technology into the curriculum.

We can assume that in many school districts across the country, not a whole lot has changed. And in the suburban community college, the scene is only slightly different. Much of the curriculum software is quite useful; instructors who have adopted it for use in the classroom have found software to be a boon to the delivery of content. Unfortunately, in affluent communities, students for whom technology is second nature outnumber teachers who are comfortable with technology. The slow pace of change that students see in their instructors is a source of frustration, and educators are equally frazzled by the speed at which they are expected to change.

The issue is not one of social inequity. It is a matter of keeping up with the pace of technology in the classroom. Simply put, students might not be getting the level of leadership and mentoring they need from teachers who can't keep up with them. Who, if not their teachers, can push young students to higher levels of learning?

Our interviews indicated two types of problems with the teacher-student relationship in the area of technology. The first and obvious concern is that younger students might have more hours and more variety of technology experience than their teachers. In fact, one interview subject commented that this has been a particular problem in his high school over the past 10 years. He was happy to report, however, that the crisis is rapidly diminishing as teachers retire and are replaced by much younger, more technologically astute instructors.

The second problem is another gap between teacher and students, this one with a slightly different twist. A college manager of technology training told us that she has experienced an all too common situation in which teachers are well qualified and certified to teach an advanced technology such as Oracle database management software. But in this case, the working adult student who comes to the college for training in this advanced, specific software has more practical hands-on experience than the teacher does in the general area of database management. The student doesn't know the specifics being taught, but he becomes frustrated on learning that he knows more than his instructor about the general subject of database management.

The Gender Wall

For a more thorough treatment of the issue of a Digital Divide between the sexes, we would point you to Chapter 8 of this book, devoted to the issue and written by Stella Perez, Cindy Miles, and Cynthia Wilson. However, since a few of our participants did identify the difference between high school boys and girls as an ongoing and important area of concern, we thought it germane to give a brief summary of our interviewees' perspectives.

Interview subjects in at least two suburban school districts observed that high school boys and high school girls approach and embrace technology in markedly different ways. The primary concern expressed by these participants is that girls are not positioning themselves to be trained and to gain experience that would help them access the lucrative career fields within technology. According to our experts, it is difficult to interest young women in computer programming, networking, repair, and engineering.

In one suburban school district, a task force is under way to study and recommend tactics for increasing the number of girls who participate in computer programming and computer engineering preparatory courses within the high school. As one person we interviewed explained, it is possible to "trick" young women into taking technology courses when the emphasis is placed on using technology as a tool for art or communication. We were told, however, that even after being tricked into technology studies, girls generally lose interest the moment the focus shifts to building networks and systems or to programming computers for data processing.

White Collar, Blue Collar

We now turn to examine suburban Digital Divides between social classes within suburban communities. Please note that this division is not the same as the simpler distinction between the affluent and the less affluent. Sociologists and marketers have long accepted the idea that there are patterns of behaviors, beliefs, and attitudes within community subcultures that can be enduring and somewhat predictable.

These subcultures do not necessarily equate to distinct differences in household income. But they do adhere to clear patterns of behavior in consumer spending, social and leisure activities, fashion, and occupations. For example, some subcultures prefer bowling to tennis. Some prefer short-sleeve polyester shirts with clip-on ties to long-sleeve cotton shirts with silk ties. Some prefer beer to wine. Some subcultures rank wild game hunting over alpine skiing. And perhaps some subcultures value technology–and benefit from its uses–more than others.

We titled this section "White Collar, Blue Collar" simply because that is how the issue was identified to us in our interviews. These are labels for two very broad social classes, with implied differences in type of work and wages received. But class structure is much more complex than that. Entire classification schemes of the American class system have been developed, ranging from the simple five-group system found in classic sociology studies to Fussell's more sophisticated nine-group system and all the way to the 40 "clusters" described by Michael Weiss (1988). We acknowledge that one of the hardest aspects of contemplating class and class differences in the U.S. is that, to many Americans, the very subject seems distasteful.

However difficult it may be to discuss social class, we must find ways to explore this possible Digital Divide. Two of our participants independently raised the issue and expressed the concern that class differences are important. They have the impression that white-collar workers value and embrace technology with more enthusiasm than blue-collar workers do, an impression apparently based on our participants' direct experiences of providing technology training courses to employees of various companies.

White-collar and blue-collar employees from the same company, even within the same factory, show strongly different attitudes toward technology. These differences in attitude, along with the many known differences among subculture behaviors, point to the possibility of a Digital Divide of some sort.

Affluent and Techno-Negative

Let's get right to the point: There are successful, affluent, socially powerful people who attempt to influence others to minimize the role of technology in their lives. Subtle though it may be, this type of antitechnology influence could have a chilling effect on progress and development. In fact, such influence has the potential to widen the Digital Divide.

We do not know the number of people who might fit this profile. Nor do we know what true and lasting effect these powerful others may have. We base our beliefs about antitech influences on a number of observable factors.

We hear, for example, of the affluent community leader who attempts to keep his college-bound children from buying personal computers, deeming them unnecessary to serious college study. We hear stories of powerful leaders who seek to minimize the role of technology in the lives of the people they influence, both at work and at home.

The idea that affluent, powerful people could cause a digital rift within their own social and family circles may seem far-fetched, but evidence convinces us that it deserves further consideration.

A Closer Look

We have presented a brief alternative view of the Digital Divide by describing several additional gaps in technology access and use, as might exist in suburban areas. The traditional view is that the Digital Divide simply mirrors other social and economic divides within our society by focusing on the relationship of race and socioeconomic status to the access and use of technology. This traditional view holds that one finds the victims of the Digital Divide in rural and poorer urban areas. While we agree that this type of divide exists and must be addressed, we have presented some less-examined breaches that are also important and that deserve further exploration.

We intend for these alternative views to augment the traditional concept of the Digital Divide, not to diminish or replace it. And we hope this discussion ultimately contributes to a fuller understanding of the complex social, academic, psychological, and economic factors related to the Digital Divide.

The authors wish to thank Sally Lahmon of Sinclair Community College for assistance with this essay.

REFERENCES

de los Santos, A. G. (2000). A Divide at Our Door: A Review of the Literature Related to the Digital Divide. In G. de los Santos, A. de los Santos, & M. Milliron (Eds.) *Access in the Information Age: Community Colleges Bridging the Digital Divide.* Mission Viejo, CA: League for Innovation in the Community College.

Fussell, P. (1983). *Class: A Painfully Accurate Guide Through the American Status System.* New York: Ballantine Books.

Tapscott, D. (1998). *Growing Up Digital: The Rise Of The Net Generation.* New York: McGraw-Hill.

Weiss, M. J. (1988). *The Clustering of America.* New York: Harper and Row.

Chapter 4

Rural Community Colleges and the Digital Divide

Sarah Butzen and Cynthia D. Liston

Since its creation, the Internet–and more broadly, information technology–has been seen as the pathway to a renaissance for rural America. With instantaneous virtual communication replacing face-to-face interactions, farm owners would now need only 40 acres and a modem and could celebrate the quality and low rents of rural life in contrast to the crowding and pollution of large cities. By bringing about the death of distance, the Internet would balance geographic inequities.

In fact, however, the opposite has taken place: the Internet and other types of electronic communication have reinforced the disadvantages of rural areas. Advanced electronic communication has become integral to almost every kind of business activity and a prerequisite for competitive advantage in nearly every industry, as well as dominating many cultural and social activities. At the same time, providers of communications services have become increasingly concentrated in urban centers whose dense markets promise a higher return on investment, shutting out rural areas from the innovations that were supposed to produce a rural renaissance.

Rural community colleges, with their access to sources of learning and technology and their close ties to their communities, are well situated to help rural areas overcome these disadvantages. What follows is an overview of the rural Digital Divide and its economic and social impact, along with some examples of ways in which rural community colleges are helping their communities embrace the potential of information technology and some recommendations on how colleges can advocate for better Internet resources and skills in their areas.

Rural Digital Divide Defined

By some measures, the rural Digital Divide is narrowing. The most recent version of *Falling Through the Net*, a series of reports on digital access from the U.S. Department of Commerce, shows that more rural people have computers and access to the Internet than ever before (NTIA, 1999). In 2000, 38.9 percent of rural households had access to the Internet, an increase from the 1998 access rate of 22.2 percent. In contrast, 42.3 percent of urban households had Internet access in 2000, a slight increase from 1998's access rate of 41.5 percent (1999). Another oft-cited study showed that 92 percent of Americans live in a county where toll-free dial-up access is available, though follow-up studies indicated that this access was often available only in the largest towns in rural counties (Strover, 1999).

But increases in access do not mean that the Digital Divide is closing. Instead, as modem access comes to rural America, more advanced forms are making basic access obsolete and creating a new Digital Divide characterized by disparity in speed, quality, and capacity of Internet access. High-speed broadband access, which is becoming the standard for both business and personal use, is much scarcer in rural areas than in urban centers. In its 2000 study of rural telecommunications, the U.S. Department of Agriculture found that broadband was available in 70 to 100 percent of cities with a population of more than 500,000; in 26 to 40 percent of cities with population between 50,000 and 250,000; in less than 5 percent of cities with population between 5,000 and 10,000; and in less than 1 percent of cities under 1,000 (U.S. Department of Agriculture, 2000).

As high-speed access becomes the norm and the majority of applications are developed solely for high-speed connections, rural users are increasingly shut out of the economic, social, and cultural benefits of the Internet. Lack of high-speed connection is a particular disadvantage to business users. Modem access provides neither the speed nor the capacity to handle most business and industrial uses, particularly e-commerce. In business use, the area of greatest economic impact, the Digital Divide is as wide as ever.

These infrastructure disparities are rooted in insufficient demonstrated demand by rural Internet users. Providers of advanced communication services are reluctant to invest in less populated areas, where their return on investment is uncertain. Yet rural markets clearly have a need for these services, even if that need is not translating effectively into demand. The digital disparities create clear disadvantages for rural areas, both economically and in rural residents' quality of life.

Economic Impact

Urban businesses are able to adopt business strategies–such as just-in-time inventory management, online customer service, and electronic marketing–that enhance the efficiency of their processes and the value of their products. Rural firms miss these opportunities and may lose business from clients who require sophisticated electronic capabilities from their suppliers. While these effects are hard to capture, one measure is that in 1998, small businesses, which drive rural economies, averaged $2.72 million in revenues, while small businesses that use the Internet averaged $3.79 million. The Small Business Administration projects that by 2003, nearly one-fourth of total business-to-business commerce will be e-commerce, from which rural businesses will largely be excluded (Williams, 2000). Further, inadequate communications infrastructure makes it less likely that new and relocating firms will choose a rural location. Telecommunications infrastructure is among the top five criteria for locating a facility (Malecki, 2001).

The economic impact of the Digital Divide is felt not only in the infrastructure, but also in the workforce. For a business to take advantage of the possibilities of e-commerce, it needs access to IT professionals who can create and maintain, for example, inventory systems and Web-based marketing strategies. But a business also needs access to a general workforce whose skill set includes sufficient computer literacy to be able to use these systems. Although it may be possible to periodically import the services of IT professionals, the everyday computer illiteracy of the existing workforce is a substantial obstacle. In many rural areas, the majority of the workforce is not computer literate, and the cost of upgrading the skills of an entire workforce is prohibitive to most employers.

Quality-of-Life Impact

The impact of the Digital Divide in rural America goes beyond economic ramifications to elements that are less tangible but nonetheless significant. The Internet created a new global world of free exchange of ideas, interests, and transactions. Whether reading movie reviews and weather reports from around the world online, participating in medical-related support sites, or taking an online course from a distant university, the Internet user enjoys amenities that in the space of less than a decade have become so vital that many people now view them as routine and available, like electricity or water service. Without affordable and reliable broadband Internet access, underserved rural populations have fewer information and connectivity options than their better-served nonrural neighbors. A USDA study cites the example of a student with broadband access taking a one-hour virtual tour of the Louvre; it would take a rural student using modem access more than 36 hours to get the same information (USDA, 2000, p. 2). Paradoxically, even though rural residents may own more land or enjoy broader vistas, their world is in fact smaller.

The divide is a personal quality-of-life issue as well as an economic one. *Remote* is even more remote when communities lack good Internet access. It is arguable that the rural Digital Divide is a destabilizing force for rural America that could be exacerbating migration to cities while at the same time discouraging individuals and families who might otherwise be attracted to the rural way of life. Conversely, when a rural community is connected, anecdotal evidence abounds of well-heeled writers, entrepreneurs, and others who seek refuge in rural areas while conducting day-to-day business with colleagues around the world through e-mail and the Internet.

Community Colleges Helping to Bridge the Divide: Benchmark Practices

In 2001, Regional Technology Strategies, Inc. published the results of a grant from the USDA's Fund for Rural America to identify benchmark practices at rural community and technical colleges in the U.S. and other countries where Internet technology has made a positive impact on local economies. Many of these practices revolve around meeting IT skill and infrastructure needs. Some of these efforts are summarized below.[1]

- Hibbing Community College (MN) runs a Community Computer Center that casts a wide net in its outreach to both businesses and the community as a whole. The center has flexible hours and distance learning that is open to the public, but also offers customized training for businesses and skill upgrading for those on public assistance.
- Garrett Community College (MD) started and then spun out a nonprofit cooperative that brought affordable Internet and Wide Area Network access to its service area for the first time. More than just meeting residents' needs for Internet access, the cooperative has been instrumental in supporting or growing companies that otherwise might have left this mountainous region.
- Community Colleges of Colorado funded its Rural E-Commerce Initiative to expand technology and education to help close the state's rural Digital Divide. Colleges in rural parts of the state are working together to offer training to firms on how to use e-commerce and to teach high school students about e-business and careers in technology.
- Walters Community Colleges, in the southern Appalachia region of Tennessee, is part of the partnership of the American Association of Community College and Microsoft called Working Connections. To expand the pipeline of IT workers, thereby enhancing the region's attractiveness to industry, the effort targets disadvantaged workers for an accelerated, intensive IT training program leading to Microsoft certification.
- Carl Sandburg College, in west central Illinois, collaborates with the local public school system and a private four-year college to operate an Educational Technology Center. The ETC encompasses a teleconference center, a 25-seat distance-learning classroom, computer classrooms offering customized training for employees, and Internet access for the general public. Customized training for 50 companies in 1999-2000 ranged from database management to customer service.

---

[1] For a complete, searchable list and profile of the practices, go to www.rtsinc.org/benchmark.

Community Colleges as Advocacy Leaders

Not surprisingly, most of the practices described here center on increasing IT skill bases in rural populations. But there are many leadership strategies by which community colleges can serve in developing long-term solutions to the Digital Divide.

Promote the Potential

Internet access and telecommunications are not always high priorities for rural residents, who may be more focused on maintaining a treasured way of life than on trying to fit the mold of an Information Society. The drive for preservation can mute a perceived demand for new services and make it difficult for those who do value these services to advocate for them. Through community forums and access to other community and business leaders, and by providing leadership to community planning efforts, community colleges can help educate rural residents and business owners about the potential benefits that advanced telecommunications services hold for rural areas.

Assess and Aggregate Demand

Many rural communities have a strong need for IT services, but the need has not yet translated into economic demand that can be seen by service providers as a signal to invest. The community college can act as a catalyst to assesses and aggregate local need for communications services. With its connections through training to many local companies, its connections through human services components to public sectors, and its access to learning and technology resources, the community college is in an ideal position to assess and aggregate demand.

Establish Partnerships

A significant element of aggregating demand is collaborating with local offices of federal agencies. Although in many rural areas these offices are the largest consumers of advanced telecommunications services, they typically use dedicated networks unavailable to the rest of the community, thus making it difficult to aggregate a sufficient level of demand to attract service providers. Community colleges are well positioned to collaborate with these agencies to capitalize on their demand for services. The agencies' networks can be extended to the entire community, or the agencies' demand for services can be aggregated with private demand through a public-private partnership that leverages federal dollars with private-sector investment. Similarly, partnerships with institutions that receive grants for digital infrastructure through the e-rate system (schools, hospitals, and libraries) could yield ways to leverage these grants with local public or private investment so that they can benefit the entire community.

Looking Ahead

Many states, especially in the West and the South, are acutely aware of the economic gulf between their urban and rural populations. The paucity of quality Internet access and the lower adoption rates of information technology in rural areas are frequently cited as sizeable barriers to economic growth. Many states have initiatives to help spur better, affordable Internet access in rural regions, and they should consider the community college as a logical lever for redress. Community colleges are well rooted in their communities and flexible in their operations and missions. With appropriate resources and partnerships, rural community colleges can be fundamental in bringing rural economies and populations better information technology links and a broader capacity to build wealth and competitive advantage.

REFERENCES

Malecki, E. (2001). Going Digital in Rural America, in Center for the Study of Rural America, *Exploring Policy Options for a New Rural America*. Kansas City: Center for the Study of Rural America, Federal Reserve Bank of Kansas City.

National Telecommunications and Information Administration. (1999). *Falling Through the Net: Defining the Digital Divide*. Washington, DC: NTIA, U.S. Department of Commerce. www.ntia.doc.gov/ntiahome/digitaldivide/.

Strover, S. (1999). Rural Internet Connectivity. Rural Policy Research Institute. www.rupri.org/pubs.archive/reports/1999/P-99-13/index.html.

U.S. Department of Agriculture. (2000). *Advanced Telecommunications in Rural America: The Challenge of Bringing Broadband Service to All Americans*. Washington, DC: U.S. Department of Agriculture. www.ntia.doc.gov/reports/ruralbb42600.pdf

Williams, V. (2000). *Small Business Expansions in Electronic Commerce*. Washington, D.C: Office of Advocacy, U.S. Small Business Administration. www.sba.gov/advo/stats/e_comm2.pdf.

CHAPTER 5

HISPANICS, THE DIGITAL DIVIDE, AND COMMUNITY COLLEGES

Alfredo G. de los Santos Jr., Ramon Dovalina, and Gerardo E. de los Santos

Hispanics are, as of 2000, the largest minority group in the United States. Since 1990, they have made significant progress in such areas as economic condition, education, and socioeconomic status. Despite this progress, gaps exist between Hispanic achievement and the population as a whole. Recent studies have shown a direct relationship between Hispanics' educational achievements and their earnings, and thus their contribution to economic development.

Hispanics: Largest Minority Group

Although Hispanics used to be known as a regional minority, the latest U.S. Census shows that they now live throughout the country, with only a few counties in some northern states of the Midwest showing no Hispanic residents.

The Hispanic population in the United States surged from 22,354,059 in 1990 to 35,305,818 in 2000, a 57.93 percent increase making them the country's largest minority group. The census reported 34,658,190 African Americans in 2000. In that year, Hispanics represented 12.5 percent of the total U.S. population (U.S. Census Bureau, *Census 2000*).

As shown in Figure 5.1, Hispanics are concentrated in five states; almost three-quarters live in California, Texas, New York, Florida, and Illinois. Nearly one-third of all Hispanics live in California, while almost one-fifth live in Texas. Close to half of all Hispanics live in these two states.

Hispanic Educational Achievement and Economic Opportunity

Figure 5.1 **Hispanics – Five Largest States, 2000**

Total number of Hispanics, 2000		35,305,818	
State	Number of Hispanics	Percent of Total Hispanics	Running Total %
California	10,966,556	31.06	31.06
Texas	6,669,666	18.89	49.95
New York	2,867,583	8.12	58.07
Florida	2,682,715	7.59	65.66
Illinois	1,530,262	4.33	69.99

While Hispanics have made some progress in educational achievement, they continue to trail behind the total population. In 1997, for example, the gap between high school graduates of all races and Hispanics was almost 20 percentage points: 62 percent for Hispanics, compared with 81.4 for all races (Wilds, p. 69).

While the college participation rate of Hispanics increased from 29 percent in 1990 to 36 percent in 1997, it was lower than that of total high school graduates: 45.2 percent (Wilds, p. 70).

The number of Hispanics enrolled in all institutions of higher education has almost doubled, from 680,000 in 1988 to 1,218,000 in 1997. Of the total Hispanics enrolled in institutions of higher education in 1997, more than half (56.6 percent) enrolled in community colleges (Wilds, p. 77).

Although Hispanics represented 14.47 percent of all 18- to 24-year-olds in 1997, they earned only 5.3 percent of the bachelor's degrees, 3.7 percent of master's, 4.8 percent of first-professional, and 3.7 percent of doctoral degrees awarded that year (Wilds, p. 30).

Only 11 percent of Hispanics 25 or older had completed four years of college in 1997, compared with 27.8 percent for all that cohort (Wilds, p. 78).

Thus the underrepresentation of Hispanics on campus and the low percentage with degrees translate into their showing in good, high-paying jobs. As a consequence, Hispanic underrepresentation on campus also translates into lower earnings. On average, White non-Hispanic men earn more than $17,000 more each year than Hispanic men; non-Hispanic women earn $6,700 a year more than Hispanic women (Carnavale, 1999).

Projections: Hispanic High School Graduation and College Enrollment

The number of Hispanics who will graduate from college is projected to increase over the next decade, from 218,358 in 1995-1996 to 517,746 by the academic year 2011-2012. By 2012, Hispanics will represent 18.7 percent of all high school graduates, compared with the 13.4 percent that African Americans will comprise that year (WICHE).

In some states, such as Arizona and New Mexico, the number of Hispanic high school graduates will exceed that of White non-Hispanics by 2012. That year in Arizona, for example, 21,980 Hispanics are projected to graduate from high school, compared with 21,468 White non-Hispanics (WICHE).

The number of Hispanic students enrolling in college will increase from 1.4 million in 1995 to 2.5 million in 2015. These 1.1 million additional Hispanic students represent a 73 percent increase. By 2006, Hispanic students are expected to outnumber African Americans enrolled in college (Carnavale, 2000, pp. 22-23).

Hispanics and the Digital Divide: Defining the Problem

Generally, there are two yardsticks for the Digital Divide: whether a household has a computer at home and whether a household has access to the Internet. By both measures, Hispanics made some progress from 1998 to 2000, but they still lagged behind the total population.

In 2000, more than one-third (33.7 percent) of all Hispanic households had a computer at home, compared with more than half of all households. These numbers contrast with 25.5 percent and 42.1 percent, respectively, in 1998. So, there was a slight narrowing of the gap in 2000 (NTIA, p. 30).

While the number of Hispanic households with access to the Internet almost doubled (from 12.6 percent in 1998 to 23.6 percent) in 2000, the gap between Hispanic households and all households was 17.9 percentage points, compared with 13.6 percentage points in 1998 (NTIA, 2000, p. 31).

Hispanic households made significant progress from 1998 to 2000, but the Digital Divide holds in the number of households with computers, and has expanded in regard to Internet access (NTIA, 2000, pp. 30-31).

Widening the Digital Divide: Wired Communities

While multiple demographic and educational data sources reveal that greater Internet access is emerging in predominantly lower-income Hispanic homes throughout the country, the rate of access continues to lag far behind that of the majority populations (NTIA, 2000, pp. xvi, 38). Coupled with the ongoing and comparatively slow rate of information access for Hispanics in the home, middle- and upper-income residents are experiencing a new kind of information access in their homes and communities, one that is unparalleled and widens on a different level the gap between those who have access and those who do not (NTIA, 2000, pp. xvi, 37).

A growing number of middle- and upper-income families are living in futuristic, master-planned communities that are redefining the use of information-technology access in the home. For example, Ladera Ranch, located in Orange County, brought the first of its kind, the *connected community*, to California. Through a partnership with a local cable access company, Ladera Ranch created the opportunity to network homes and access a community Intranet that enables neighbors to connect in revolutionary new ways.

As a wired community, Ladera Ranch enjoys an infrastructure that enables online residents to stay connected with community schools, medical facilities, businesses, and each other through high-speed Internet service, which offers a single source provider for all video, voice, and data communications needs (www.laderaranch.com, 2001). Ladera Ranch homes feature state-of-the-art structured wiring, designed to offer flexible network options, including the following:

- High-speed Internet access to every room of every home

- Option to watch one video image on all televisions connected to the home's networked system

- Ability to network all computers, printers, and scanners with the use of a cable modem, ethernet hub, and ethernet card

- Opportunity for homeowners to call in to their home's wiring from a remote location to activate lights, exterior irrigation systems, and alarm systems, and a multitude of other functions (www.laderaranch.com, 2001)

In addition to the wired network opportunities, Ladera Ranch residents benefit from a community Intranet that offers an exclusive range of capabilities, including the following:

- Online linkage to neighbors, local businesses, and community activities

- Self-publishing

- Connectivity to start or participate in new clubs, teams, and resident-inspired events (for example, the All Girls Club, the Golf Club, or Mommy and Me), or to find a babysitter or walking partner

- A direct link to Ladera Ranch Community Services' calendar of events (www.laderaranch.com, 2001)

Technology-friendly homes and communities are emerging all over the country and are redefining home access opportunities to computers, the Internet, and now community intranets. These cutting-edge, connected communities are leap-frogging previous generations of technology in the home through new and innovative partnerships with local cable and network community partners. Home information access already far surpasses the basic technological access options of the average Hispanic resident and other predominantly lower-income families (NTIA, 2000, pp. 30-31).

Community College Response to the Digital Divide

Community colleges across the country are responding to the Digital Divide by creating partnerships with community groups, local and state agencies, public school systems, and corporate partners. The responses of two community colleges–Santa Ana College and Laredo Community College–are included here as examples.

Santa Ana College: Neighborhood Technology Center

Santa Ana, California, is a city of 315,000 residents, of whom 238,621, or 76 percent, are Hispanic. Working with the Santa Ana Unified School District, the City of Santa Ana, Orange County Board of Supervisors, AhaPlanet.com, and several community organizations, Santa Ana College dedicated its first Neighborhood Technology Center (NTC) in April 2001. The Chancellor's Office of California Community Colleges funds the NTC.

Located off campus at the Mexican American Opportunity Foundation, the NTC provides free computer instruction to adult immigrants, single parents, and unemployed and underemployed workers, right in their own neighborhoods.

The intent is for the center to serve as a replicable model where the community college, in concert with local businesses and organizations, can develop a blueprint for other sites to be replicated throughout California. One of two colleges in the Rancho Santiago Community College District, Santa Ana is planning a second center.

A Hispanic Community and the Digital Divide: Laredo, Texas

If there is a Digital Divide between the ethnic majority population and minorities in America, surely Laredo, Texas, must be in the deepest abyss. With some 95 percent Hispanics in its metropolitan statistical population of almost 200,000, Laredo is among the most minority of communities in the United States. Moreover, Laredo sits along the border between the United States and Mexico, and its sister city of Nuevo Laredo has an estimated population of over 600,000.

Laredo is a community that has addressed the issue of the Digital Divide for its citizens. The city, community college, school districts, and other entities in the community and the region have combined their resources and partnered in a distinctive way to bring the area into the 22nd century with technology. The area can serve as a model for other minority communities.

Laredo is a community of contrasts. The international border and the Rio Grande are, to Laredoans, merely artificial barriers, as thousands of Mexicans and Americans cross this inland port to shop, visit family members, play, work, attend school, and conduct business. It is a vibrant community, voted an All-American city. For more than a decade, only Las Vegas has surpassed Laredo in growth.

As the country's largest inland port, Laredo leads the nation in overland import-export traffic. In the year 2000, Laredo port traffic accounted for the following dynamics:

Pedestrian crossings	9,053,717
Railroad crossings	335,608
Vehicle crossings	16,339,383
Truck crossings	2,902,409
U.S. exports to Mexico	$39.3 billion
U.S. Imports from Mexico	$45.5 billion

Not surprisingly, tourism, transportation, and international business are in the city's center of commerce and employment. But Laredo has its problems.

Unemployment and underemployment, poverty, housing problems, drugs, environmental concerns, health issues, and low levels of education are major worries for this area. Webb County, which encompasses Laredo, is the fifth largest county in the state by area, yet it is one of its poorest. One in every three families lives at or below the poverty level. Over half of the adult population has not completed high school.

The high incidence of at-risk students and high dropout rates are chronic problems. More than 25,000 adults have not completed their education past the 9th grade. Only 48.8 percent of adults have completed high school, compared with the still-low state level of 77.1 percent. More than half of the population has limited English proficiency. One in every four adults is illiterate in both English and Spanish.

The level of unemployment is chronically much higher than the state average; after many years of double-digit unemployment, the unemployment rate finally dropped to 6.4 percent in the recent, healthier economic period of the late 1990s.

In this vibrant but contrasted city of heavy international commerce and high poverty rates, 50,116 people live below the poverty threshold. The majority of the community earns between $15,000 and $24,999 per year. Figure 5.2 indicates the income breakdown for Webb County.

Figure 5.2 **Community Income Categories–Webb County, Texas**

Community Income Categories	
Income Levels	# Residents
Less than $5,000	4,992
$5,000 to $9,999	4,992
$10,000 to $14, 999	4,781
$15,000 to $24, 999	6,951
$25,000 to $34, 999	4,829
$35,000 to $40, 999	4,169
$50,000 to $74, 999	2,236
$75,000 to $99,999	833
$100,000 to $149,000	418
$150,000 or more	309

Other significant data for the community indicate that

- the rate for contracting tuberculosis is twice that of the State of California;
- the mortality rate from diabetes is nearly twice that of the State of Texas;
- obesity rates are 50 percent above the state average;
- heart disease strikes 40 percent more often than the national average; and
- breast cancer incidence is 60 percent higher than the national average.

Laredo, then, is a community with a diverse population, and one of international importance. It is at the center of trade and of a population in transition. It is a community with a panoply of assets and an even larger and growing pool of needs.

Given the problems, disseminating information to constituents or customers is vital to the different governmental agencies, and access to that information through the Internet becomes critically important to the citizens being served.

One might infer that the general population lacks access to new technology, modern telecommunications, and information systems. However, though individuals may lack personal access to computers and technology in the home (and even then the Digital Divide varies tremendously from suburbs to barrios and from the haves to the have-nots within the community), the educational systems in the community have addressed those needs and collaborated with other entities to provide that access.

The city, the county, the community college, the school districts within the community college's service area, community and recreational centers, and the hospital and medical centers have worked together and alongside their counterparts throughout the state to bring education, information, and technology access to their constituents. Laredo is indeed an example for other minority communities.

Laredo Community College as a Technology Leader

Since 1947, Laredo Community College has been serving the Laredo area with the programs and services normally associated with a comprehensive community college: associate degree transfer programs, degree and certificate workforce programs, adult and continuing education, and the necessary support services. The college served 7,500 college-credit students in the 2001 fall semester. Some 3,000 others attended adult and continuing education classes. Like the community it serves, the college is predominately Hispanic, the most Hispanic higher education institution in the United States, except for those in Puerto Rico. Nearly 96 percent of its students are minorities, predominantly Hispanic. A nine-member board, all Hispanic, governs the college; its chief executive officer is also Hispanic. It is the only such institution in the country.

In 1995, as the result of a court settlement between the city and Time-Warner Communications, the City of Laredo began developing a fiber-optic loop to connect its various city departments in the community. The community college and the school districts also benefited, because the loop connected the high schools and the college to the loop and to each other. From this initial extraordinary funding source grew a fast-paced developmental period of infusion of technology and technology-driven services. The change also created, out of necessity, an unparalleled series of partnerships and collaborative approaches for addressing technology needs in the community. In addition to the partnerships, each entity has sought and obtained further funding from external sources to complement the partnerships and close the Digital Divide.

Laredo Community College quickly recognized that the majority of low-income residents lived in South Laredo, away from its historic campus, and in the *colonias* away from the city proper. The *colonias*–rural and isolated third-world neighborhoods–lacked access to basic infrastructure necessities such as water, electricity, and sewer systems. Obviously, access to information resources and technology were beyond a dream for these residents.

Because of limited public transportation, isolation was even greater than for other residents. Like the *colonia* residents, who were isolated from city and county services, so were the educational, medical, governmental, and business entities isolated from other similar entities. Laredo and Nuevo Laredo are fully 150 miles from other major metropolitan centers, such as San Antonio to the north and Monterrey to the south.

Laredo needed a planning process and a collaborative approach to take stock of its community resources and to integrate them into one system. The possible partners had common needs: to share resources, to share information, to connect with each other and with constituents, and to do all of these efficiently.

Since that initial planning and action, the community college has collaborated with 12 other regional agencies to form the first locally planned and managed telecommunications system for a four-county area of south Texas. Through funding from the Texas Infrastructure Fund, the United States Department of Commerce, local taxes, and private venture, the partnership has linked colleges, schools, libraries, and medical facilities to each other and to the Internet in ways that could only have been dreamed of seven years earlier. The system now focuses primarily on information sharing and education. Chiefly, it addresses student access to technology and distance education.

Apart from the initial funding from Time-Warner, the Texas Infrastructure Fund Board (TIF) has been the most critical source for funding support. Without the fund, the partnership accomplishments would not have been possible. According to the TIF Web page (www.tifb.state.tx.us), the Board had its beginnings with the launching of the 1993 federal initiative, the National Information Infrastructure (NII). One research expert remarked that it "ranks with the space race as a major technology-centered policy initiative." In a government publication cited on the same Web page, the objectives of the NII are spelled out:

> The administration's vision is of . . . networks that will help America to prepare its children for the workplace of the 21st century, allow all Americans to continue their education . . . extend . . . medical care to remote rural areas . . . and make America's businesses the most competitive in the world. The president has challenged the nation to connect all of its schools, libraries, and hospitals to the information superhighway by the year 2000.

The TIF was created in May 1995, when then-Governor George Bush signed House Bill 2128, also referred to as PURA '95, the Public Utility Regulatory Act of 1995. PURA '95 advances several important policies of the state as well as regulating the public utilities. It stresses the modernization of the technology infrastructure for schools, libraries, and health care facilities. According to TIF, its specific charge is to

> help develop the telecommunications infrastructure that connects public entities such as public schools, public libraries, two- and four-year colleges and universities, and the public health delivery system in Texas. A nine-member board of directors that is charged with disbursing approximately $1.5 billion in revenues through loans and a formal grant program governs TIF.

Figure 5.3 lists the grants secured by Laredo Community College for technology enhancements.

Figure 5.3 Telecommunication Grant Funds Received

Award Date	Funding Agency	Funded Amount	Purpose
9/1/96	SBC Southwestern Bell	$75,000	$25,000 per year for 3 years: Training for media and technology staff
2/24/97	UISD/LISD/Zapata ISD	$75,000	Distance Learning Pilot Project $25,000.00 each (LISD, UISD, ZISD)
5/29/97	Sony	$4,500	Staff Development - ongoing $4,000 - 3/24/98 $500 - 5/29/97
8/26/97	University of Texas Health Science Center (UTHSC)	$8,127	Distance Learning Project
9/1/97	UTHSC	$80,000	$40,000 per year for 2 years Distance Learning Project
10/1/97	U.S. Department of Commerce - TIIAP	$586,620	Project Salud - distance learning, pre-med courses at high school level, public health information
7/1/98	TIFB Internet	$257,200	LCC Corral – Internet access for 60 students
1/4/99	TIFB	$1,000,000	Discovery - distance learning, health awareness and health career preparation
10/31/00	TIFB (CN1) Community Networking	$500,000	NOSOTROS Net, an Internet-based community network
07/30/01	TIFB (LB8) Library Grant	$151,910	Funds to upgrade library research services and Internet access
07/30/01	TIFB (HE3) Higher Education	$188,518	Funds for teacher certification and distance education equipment and software

In the last six years, Laredo Community College has become one of the most wired community colleges in the country. Its distance education division provides interactive classes and online courses and programs through its access channel, TV-55. The college is also connected to the other 49 community college districts through the Virtual College of Texas, which allows any student in any Texas community college to enroll for Internet courses at any other Texas college. Every faculty member goes through computer literacy classes and, on completion, is provided with a personal computer.

Students have Internet access thanks to 43 computer labs with over a thousand computers, including research access in the library and a computer "Corral" (the former student activity center) with 60 computers. The college has purchased over 1,500 computers in the last six years.

Laredo Independent School District

Laredo Independent School District (LISD) consists of 21 elementary schools, four middle schools, three high schools, and two magnet schools, and has a current enrollment of over 24,000 students. It serves the older part of the city and follows the old city limits. According to district officials, only 5 percent of the district's students enjoy computer access at home. For that reason, the district master plan has promoted Internet access in schools.

Along with grant purchases, the district had a lease agreement with Dell Computer Corporation for 2,500 personal computers. When the contract ended in 2001, and new computers were secured, the district had an option to buy the old computers at 10 percent of their original value. Instead, the district opted to make the computers available to faculty and students for a mere $165 each.

The high schools are also using campus funds to buy laptops and allowing their students to check them out. Thanks to a federal challenge grant and a partnership with Highland Park ISD near Dallas, computer literacy classes are also being offered at four schools. The parents have access to laptops that can be checked out.

The district's schools are connected to its distance learning network, as is the LISD main office. The district has a website, Internet access for students, its own television studio and cable television access, and teleconferencing capabilities.

Figure 5.4 lists other grants that have been secured by the district to address its technology needs.

Figure 5.4 **LISD Grants Active 2001-2002**

Grant Source	Grant ID Number	Grant Period	Description	Campuses	Amount
U.S. Dept. of Education Challenge Grant	Project KIDS	08/1999 to 07/2004	Grant with Allen ISD	3 elementary schools, 1 middle school, and 1 high school	$200,000
Texas Infrastructure Fund	PS8	10/02/2000 to 12/31/2001	336 workstations for educators, distance learning equipment, library automation	4 middle schools and 3 high schools	$597,964
Texas Infrastructure Fund	LB5	10/02/2000 to 09/28/2001	Library automation for Cigarroa and Martin High Schools	2 high schools	$70,000
Intel & Microsoft		03/01/2001 to 05/31/2002	Resources such as lessons online, training for teachers	All schools	$97,500
Texas Infrastructure Fund	PS9	05/15/2001 to 08/14/2002	Wireless labs	6 elementary schools	$240,000

United Independent School District

Made up of 21 elementary schools, seven middle schools, and four high schools, UISD has a total enrollment of over 25,000 students and is the fastest growing district in the state. The district surrounds the LISD and covers 2,448 square miles, an area the size of the state of Delaware.

Through the support of TIF, the Texas Education Agency, and local tax revenues, UISD has a well-developed technology infrastructure. Recent innovations include technology-enhanced curricula in the 4th and 5th grades; the district is also providing students with wireless keyboards. The wireless system provides a typing tutor, word processing with up to 70 pages of text, 10 different folders, and infrared transfer. The middle schools also have an online curriculum, and an innovative distance learning center focusing on health and science education is located at Alexander High School.

UISD has a website, Internet access for students, and teleconferencing equipment. Technology projects for 2001-2002 include wireless connectivity to 52 portable buildings, IP Telephony for the new high school, Microsoft certification and Cisco Academies at all high schools, and Web pages for every school in the district.

Figure 5.5 indicates the district's most recent funding for technology.

***Figure 5.5* UISD Technology Funding**

YEAR	PURPOSE	SOURCE	AMOUNT
1999-2000	Upgrade 3 high schools' network infrastructure	1998 Bond Project	$383,756
1999-2000	Network equipment and computer stations for 4 elementary schools	1998 Bond Project	$222,240
2000-2001	Upgrade network infrastructure in 7 middle schools	1998 Bond Project	$565,073
2000-2001	Computer equipment and software application for new high school	1998 Bond Project	$441,600
2000-2001	Internet	TEA	$52,000
2000-2001	Technology Grant I	TIF	$320,000
2000-2001	Technology Innovation	TEA	$750,000
2000-2001	Technology Grant II	TIF	$650,000
2000-2001	Project Millennium	U.S. Dept. of Education	$9,600,000

Mercy Health Systems of Texas

A beneficiary of TIF funding through a recent telemedicine grant, Mercy Health Systems (MHS) is the major medical and health service provider for the region. MHS recently moved to a new $130 million facility for its headquarters, and has the benefit of a $10 million technology infrastructure with Internet and WAN connectivity to all Mercy Hospitals nationwide. MHS has Internet connections for over 1,000 PCs, teleconferencing equipment, telemedicine (including direct patient care), and an Internet-based diabetes management system (Home Hero) funded by the TIF Board.

Other Partners

The City of Laredo Library has Internet connections for public use and is a site for community college classes. The Laredo Chamber of

Commerce has a website and is accessible through the Internet and e-mail. The Workforce Development Board is accessible through e-mail and has a website under development. The Workforce Development Board offers job-search assistance, entry-level skill training, literacy classes, and employment training for community members. The City of Laredo has a website, Internet access, and a fiber-optics network called Inet. The Laredo Public Library and the public-access cable TV channels are included under the umbrella of city government.

Webb County has four Internet service providers: Southwestern Bell Telephone, Netscorp, Surfus, and ICSI Net. Southwestern Bell Telephone also provides ISDN, T-1, DS-3, and ADSL lines. Time-Warner Communications and Heartland Communications provide cable TV service.

A Model for Minorities

Because of lower education and socioeconomic levels in the adult population, many Hispanic parents and students lack access to new technology, modern telecommunications, and information systems. Community colleges and public school districts have a responsibility to their students to compensate for this lack of access.

Through grants and gifts, through collaboration, and through partnerships with governmental agencies, the education systems can put together an elaborate and successful technology infrastructure with the necessary supporting systems. Laredo serves as a model for other minority communities.

REFERENCES

Carnavale, A. P., & Fry, R. A. (2000). *Crossing the Great Divide: Can We Achieve Equity When Generation Y Goes to College?* Princeton, NJ: Educational Testing Service.

Carnavale, A. P. (1999). *Education=Success: Empowering Hispanic Youth and Adults.* Princeton, NJ: Educational Testing Service.

National Telecommunications and Information Administration. (2000). *Falling Through the Net: Toward Digital Inclusion.* Washington, DC: U.S. Department of Commerce.

U.S. Bureau of the Census. (2000). *Census 2002.* Washington, DC: U.S. Department of Commerce.

Western Interstate Commission for Higher Education and The College Board (1998). *Knocking at the College Door.* Boulder, CO: WICHE Publications.

Wild, D. J. (2000). *Minorities in Higher Education: Seventeenth Annual Status Report.* Washington, DC: American Council on Education.

Authors' Note: Neiel W. Wohlers, Jr., Grant Development Officer at Laredo Community College; Carmen S. Sandoval, Administrative Assistant for Instructional Technology at Laredo Independent School District; and Alicia Carrillo, Career and Technology Education Director at United Independent School District contributed information for the portion of this article on Laredo and Laredo Community College. Rita Cepeda, President of Santa Ana College, provided information about the College's Neighborhood Technology Center.

CHAPTER 6

WE HAVE THE HOOK-UP:
DEVELOPING EFFECTIVE TECHNOLOGY PROGRAMS
FOR THE AFRICAN-AMERICAN COMMUNITY

Henry D. Shannon and Ron C. Smith

First, the good news: Computer technology and the Internet have opened a world of opportunities, making it easier than ever to explore and learn about virtually any topic. We can travel around the globe, communicating with people across the ocean without even leaving our desks. We can pay our bills electronically and not have to lick any stamps. We can purchase holiday gifts online and let others battle the crowds at shopping centers. We can access conveniences and information that our grandparents would hardly have imagined, simply by clicking a mouse and tapping our keyboards.

Now for the bad news: Not everyone has access to the same world of opportunities. Some Americans face a Digital Divide, the gap that separates the information haves from the have-nots. These information have-nots include certain minority groups, low-income persons, the less educated, and children of single-parent households, particularly when they reside in rural areas or central cities. Former U.S. Assistant Secretary of Commerce Gregory L. Rohde talked of these have-nots with participants in a Dec. 9, 1999 conference on the Digital Divide. They are shut out, Rohde said, from the technology jobs of our new information-based economy because they lack computer skills. They are unable to take advantage of the educational, financial, and shopping opportunities of a wired world. In short, they are at an increasing disadvantage because they lack access to–and the skills to use–the technology tools that most of us take for granted every day.

Technology's ability to create an underclass is a familiar story for members of the African-American community. In the early 20th century, more than 90 percent of the African-American population lived in the South, and most earned their incomes in the agricultural fields. Their jobs evaporated after a mechanical cotton picker that could do the work of 50 people was introduced in 1944, and more than five million Black men, women, and children migrated north in search of work. Some African Americans found unskilled jobs in manufacturing plants. Once again, those unskilled workers were hit hard when companies began to automate their factories to save money. Millions of unskilled Black workers and their families became part of an urban underclass that lives a marginal existence of unemployment and poverty.

We've learned the lesson that technology can create an underclass of have-nots. It is our responsibility to stop history from repeating itself, and to provide access to the skills and resources to which everyone is entitled in today's techno-savvy world.

The Gap

Just how wide is the Digital Divide between African Americans and nonminority Americans? *Toward Digital Inclusion: a Report on America's Access to Technology Tools* chronicles the gap. The U.S. Department of Commerce, the Economics and Statistics Administration, and the National Telecommunications and Information Administration released the report in October 2000.

As of August 2000, 23.5 percent of Black households had home access to the Internet, compared with 41.5 percent of households nationally. The gap between African Americans and households nationally that have Internet access is growing. While about a third of the U.S. population uses the Internet at home, only 18.9 percent of African Americans access the Internet from their homes.

Income has a direct bearing on whether African Americans have Internet access. Households earning more than $75,000 are more likely to have Internet access, with the gap between African Americans and Caucasian Americans narrowing at 70.9 percent and 78.6 percent, respectively. The percentage of African-American households earning below $15,000 that have Internet access plummets to 6.4 percent.

What about computer ownership? About 51 percent of the households nationally own computers, compared with 32.6 percent of African-American households. That represents a gap of 18.4 percentage points, which has not narrowed. As with Internet access, the gap between computer ownership of White and Black households narrows as the income level increases. Among households earning more than $75,000, 87 percent of Whites and 83.4 percent of Blacks own computers. And at incomes of less than $15,000, 11.5 percent of Black households and 22.8 percent of White households are likely to own computers.

Although Internet access and computer ownership are rising for almost all groups, a Digital Divide remains and, in some cases, is even getting worse. While progress has occurred, much work remains to be done. We must continue to expand access to technology tools if we have any hopes of bridging the Digital Divide.

St. Louis Community College's Role

St. Louis Community College (SLCC) has stepped up to meet the challenge of bridging the Digital Divide, particularly between African Americans and nonminorities. It has targeted African Americans because they represent the region's largest minority group. As an institution of teaching and learning, part of SLCC's mission is to lead the way in responding to the multiple educational and training needs of its diverse community. To pretend that the Digital Divide is imaginary would be shirking responsibility to its constituents.

St. Louis Community College is the largest community college system in Missouri and one of the largest in the United States. It serves some 130,000 credit and noncredit students each year, and ranks among the top 20 community colleges in the number of graduates. SLCC has three main campuses–Meramec in southwest St. Louis County, Florissant Valley in north St. Louis County, and Forest Park in the City of St. Louis–and four major off-campus centers. They share a commitment to providing educational excellence at an affordable price. St. Louis Community College's Forest Park campus–and its community outreach facility, the William J. Harrison Northside Education Center, in a predominately African-American neighborhood of St. Louis, form the hub of many programs designed to narrow the Digital Divide. SLCC measures its success not only by the numbers of people it reaches, but also by the impact its services have on the lives of individual community members.

Computer Education: A Key to Welfare-to-Work Training

Bonnie was almost in tears when she arrived for her first Computer Office Skills class at the William J. Harrison Northside Education Center (HEC). A recipient of Temporary Assistance for Needy Families (TANF), she had been referred to Welfare-to-Work training by Mother's Way Career Counseling.

But as Bonnie looked around at the 19 other women–all poised in front of computers–she was overwhelmed, intimidated by the prospect of trying to learn the new technology. She believed she was the only one in the room with no clue about what she was doing in a computer lab.

By the end of the first week of computer training, Bonnie, who was in her late 20s, had a goal, and she saw that it was within her reach. She vowed to become proficient at keyboarding and at using standard office computer programs like Microsoft Word, Excel, Access, and PowerPoint.

Bonnie became unstoppable. She worked ahead on assignments, had boundless energy, and was highly motivated to achieve. When St. Louis Public Schools called the Harrison Education Center in search of someone who could work as a temporary secretary, there was no hesitation in referring Bonnie. She fit the bill perfectly, and now she is earning a respectable salary with the opportunity to advance. Best of all, Bonnie is just one example of SLCC's success.

The Computerized Office Skills Job Training Program at Harrison Education Center is among the examples of how St. Louis Community College is bridging the Digital Divide between African Americans and nonminorities. It consists of eight weeks of intensive classroom study. Students are in class five hours a day, learning the skills they need to work in a modern office environment. They learn keyboarding, Windows, Microsoft Word, Access, Excel, and PowerPoint. SLCC also teaches business English and business math, and offers life- and job-skills training. While the computer is the focus of the program, SLCC teaches all the basic skills that employees need to be productive in the workplace.

After the eight weeks of formal training, students spend four weeks working as interns in offices. SLCC has a partnership with the St. Louis Public Schools' Human Resource Division that places students at one of the public schools. The Internal Revenue Service, Community Health-In-Partnership Services (CHIPS), Grand Rock Economic Development Corporation, and Ralston Purina are among the members of the business sector that have offered internships. Many have hired students after they completed these internships.

The Computerized Office Skills Job Training Program is growing. In Fiscal Year 1999-2000, 30 students participated in the program. The following year, it served 42 participants, representing a nearly 30 percent increase. About 60 percent of those students now have jobs, typically earning between $17,000 and $18,000 in upwardly mobile positions that would have been beyond their reach without training.

SLCC's arrangement with Mother's Way Career Counseling, in addition to its work with business partners, is a key to the program's success. The college teams with agencies that are accepted and trusted by members of its African-American community. Additionally, because Harrison Education Center is in the midst of the community SLCC wants to serve, its presence shows that the college is a stakeholder in the success of that community.

Training at Community Institutions

Another way SLCC uses partnerships to bridge the Digital Divide between the African-American and nonminority communities is by taking its training on the road. St. Louis Community College instructors offer computer training in a variety of venues. The college has a partnership with the St. Louis Public Library to conduct computer classes at three of the library's branch locations. Classes are free to any resident of the City of St. Louis who holds a library card. Often, training introduces an individual to the opportunities that computers provide and becomes a student's first connection with the Internet. For the first year of the program, Fiscal Year 2000-2001, SLCC conducted nearly 200 seminars for more than 2,000 students.

The college also has offered computer classes at well-respected institutions that serve young people in the community. At the Herbert Hoover Boys and Girls Club, SLCC teaches the computer component of a 10-week summer camp for 450 children ages 5 through 18. The facility has a state-of-the-art computer lab that is open during the summer and after-school hours. Many children have set up e-mail accounts; they use computers at the club to access the Internet and design PowerPoint presentations. The college offers a different computer course at the Mathews-Dickey Boys and Girls Club.

During two 20-week sessions, SLCC taught computer skills to adults. Half of the students in one class immediately purchased computers to take their skills to the next level. The college also reached those who work directly with Mathews-Dickey's young constituency, giving them pointers on assisting young people in a computer classroom setting. SLCC has conducted computer classes for adults and young people at the Youth and Family Center, an agency in the low-income north side of St. Louis that offers before- and after-school programs for families.

Family Computer Ownership Program

Learning the skills to operate a computer is only part of the solution to bridging the Digital Divide. Families need to have computers in their homes so they can use them whenever necessary to build a budget, pay bills, do homework, write letters, or search for a job. The computer has become a basic tool in our lives.

Through an innovative program sponsored by Grand Rock Community Economic Development Corporation, St. Alphonsus "Rock" Church, and the Blumeyer Village Tenant Association, families who live in the 18th and 19th Wards of St. Louis can attend 10 weeks of computer training and earn a computer when their classes end. The Danforth Foundation and Anheuser-Busch Companies, Inc. have funded the initiative. Between 85 and 90 percent of the families who enroll finish the courses. After the program's first two years of operation, 85 families who otherwise could not have afforded computers acquired them for their homes.

During the Saturday morning sessions, children often spearhead the learning and motivate their parents to excel. And the program has other unanticipated benefits. For instance, neighbors who were strangers become friends and now watch out for each other. Some adults who attended the classes were so impressed by the patience and knowledge of the instructor that they felt comfortable enrolling as students at St. Louis Community College at Forest Park.

Cloteria is one of many for whom the Digital Divide has narrowed dramatically. She attended the computer classes with her 12-year-old daughter Khalidah and discovered that having a computer in her home simplified her job search. Without having to wait in line to use a computer at the library, she could easily write cover letters and update her résumé and biography.

Cloteria now has a job as a customer service representative, a position that uses the computer office skills she learned in the training program. Meanwhile, Khalidah, who had been a good student before, has become an excellent student. She uses the Internet as an encyclopedia to augment her classroom studies. Having a computer opened up new worlds for the family.

Cisco Academy

In addition to addressing the technology gap through training programs at its educational outreach center and at various community agencies, SLCC is working on the problem at its Forest Park campus. One initiative received national recognition in May 2000 when it was selected by the U.S. Department of Housing and Urban Development as one of 10 pilot programs that demonstrate best practices in bridging the Digital Divide between nontraditional and traditional populations.

SLCC set up a Cisco Networking Academy in 1998 to train juniors and seniors from Vashon High School, which is located in a low-income neighborhood and serves mostly African-American students. The students earn college credit by taking courses that teach them how to design, build, and maintain computer networks.

As the market leader for Internet routers and related networking equipment, Cisco Systems, Inc. recognized a shortage of people capable of filling information technology positions. The company developed the training program to teach the necessary skills. Academy graduates who pass the industry-standard certification exam are immediately eligible for more than 800,000 unfilled technology jobs, many of which command high starting salaries. Of the 12 Vashon students who completed the first Cisco program, all are attending college.

Essence was one of those students. She graduated as valedictorian of her Vashon High School class and received a full scholarship to continue her education in information technology at St. Louis Community College at Forest Park.

The program–a collaboration among the college, Cisco, St. Louis Public Schools, Missouri Department of Elementary and Secondary Education, and St. Louis Enterprise Community–was so successful that SLCC expanded it. The college is now a Cisco Regional Networking Academy. This signifies that it is authorized to train the instructors who will teach Cisco Academies in their computer labs at 11 local high schools and a neighboring community college. In this way, SLCC is having an impact on an even greater number of people who otherwise might have slipped into the Digital Divide.

Open Doors

As one of the largest community colleges in the nation, SLCC is committed to developing strategies to help narrow the technology gap between members of the African-American and nonminority communities. Its success is built on a strong partnership of collaboration and coordination among well-established and respected community groups and associations. Because the college hooks into existing institutions, it receives instant access and credibility in extending its reach to African Americans.

SLCC's efforts have opened the door to higher education for students who would not have considered the option before. Some participants in its outreach programs have continued their education at St. Louis Community College because they felt comfortable with the instructors who taught their training programs. A well-educated, skilled workforce is good news for everyone in the community.

But most important, SLCC's work in bridging the Digital Divide is so rewarding because it offers students hope. Whether they are 6-year-olds at Herbert Hoover Boys and Girls Club, seniors at Vashon High School, or TANF recipients who want to break the cycle of poverty, SLCC's students understand that technology skills can help them realize the potential for a better life. That hope, and the perspective that the future will be brighter, can propel underserved members of the community toward success and achievement.

REFERENCES

Rifkin, J. African Americans and Automation: How Technology Created the Urban Underclass. *Utne Reader.* May-June, 1995.

Rohde, G. *Closing the Digital Divide.* Internet: June 30, 2001. http://www/digitaldivide.gov/summit/rohdestatement.html.

U.S. Department of Commerce, National Telecommunications and Information Administration. Falling Through the Net: *Toward Digital Inclusion.* Internet: July 1, 2001. http:www.ntia.doc.gov/ntiahome/digitaldivide.

CHAPTER 7

TECHNOLOGICAL INNOVATION VIA EDUCATION: SOME GUIDELINES FOR BUILDING PARTNERSHIPS WITH TRIBAL COMMUNITIES

William W. Erdly and Dianne Bissell

Technology is often heralded as the solution to many of the challenges facing underserved populations as they strive to achieve a variety of cultural, educational, and economic goals. Unfortunately, without an effective strategy and committed leadership, technology often fails. And that apparent failure of technology may be attributed to the wrong technological solution used to solve the problem, feature or scope creep resulting in cost overruns, poor software and hardware selection processes resulting in user-unfriendly applications, failure to recognize and understand the impact of cultural differences, and poor educational planning. These barriers need to be overcome so that access and technology-literacy issues may be addressed. In fact, the very process of overcoming these barriers may lead to increased technology literacy and improved access.

Many of the lessons learned from technology implementations served as the inspiration for the development of a partnership between the Tulalip Tribes, Everett Community College (EvCC), and the University of Washington, Bothell (UWB). The Tulalip Tribes desired an integrated information system that serves all tribal members and employees, and also that can provide access to services and data important to external entities. After several early glances at independent contractors and other organizations, the Tulalip Tribes looked toward the educational community for technical guidance and educational support in reaching their goal. They felt that this project was first and foremost an incredible learning opportunity that would have long-lasting benefits for the entire region and would help bridge the Digital Divide.

Preserving the Past, Building a Future: A Vision for the Tulalip Tribes

The first meeting between EvCC, UWB, and the Tulalip Tribes could be described as unbelievable, in a very positive way. An executive from the tribes arrived at the meeting and identified a short list of tasks that needed some support:

- Build a network and telecommunications infrastructure for a 22,000-acre reservation.
- Design systems to manage and store a variety of data and multimedia content.
- Put information systems in place to enhance tribal communications.
- Foster managed growth in business and economic development.
- Enhance educational opportunities for tribal families.
- Preserve the culture (customs, art, history, and language).
- Facilitate the social, health, and economic well-being of the Tulalip Tribes.
- Develop a technology infrastructure to be managed and owned by tribal members.
- Provide education and training to ensure a skilled workforce is in place to build and maintain these systems.

Our initial response as educators was stunned silence. We were struck by the complexities involved in these requests. We were then asked to propose a way to partner with the Tulalip Tribes to achieve these goals. UWB and EvCC devised a plan that would leverage the combined strengths of the university and community college and, most important, benefit students and tribal members alike. In view of the scope and complexities of the project, expertise in tribal culture, technology, local government, private business, K-20 education, and fiscal management were required to address the challenge. Only through a teaming approach that leveraged a wide multiplicity of knowledge domains would this important project have a chance. This approach resulted in an organization we would call Tulalip Technology Leap (TTL)–an apt name, as we were truly leaping into the future.

Getting There by Being There

The tribal council chartered the TTL team to complete a detailed needs analysis and strategy for implementing new information technologies. This included a baseline analysis of the infrastructure requirements and process needs of the Tulalip Tribes. Essential tasks included mapping out floor plans of shared community building spaces, assessing the existing networking and telecommunications systems, and finding ways to simplify data collection, storage, management, and report dissemination.

To complete these initial tasks, the TTL team needed to have a physical presence on site. Staff, students, tribal employees, and members needed a place to meet and learn about each other rather than sit in isolation at their campus computers. The TTL Coordinating Center, located on the reservation, was set up to serve as a work and meeting place. Existing computers and electrical systems in the facility were upgraded, and additional hardware and software were purchased to meet the project's computing and document-management needs. Budget, contracts, and operating procedures were established jointly by all partnering organizations in a timely and efficient manner. The budget and overhead expenses are carefully controlled and kept to a minimum, with the community college serving as the fiscal agent until the project becomes fully managed by the tribes.

The TTL team interviewed and worked directly with over 40 tribal representatives from such areas as education, business, government, social and health services, cultural preservation, natural resources, and households within the Tulalip community to identify significant needs. After the initial interviews were completed, we were amazed to uncover over 170 ideas for technology projects, all generated by tribal members and the TTL team. We are certain that many more ideas will be generated as we continue to work with tribal members.

Our longer-term strategy, once the network infrastructure and support services are in place, is to deploy critical technology applications that have direct benefits as identified by tribal interests. These applications may include e-learning for K-12, enhancing job skills and opportunities for the under- and unemployed, fostering hope in the form of alternatives for economic development, and capturing the richness of the art, language, and culture of the past. Several of these projects may be able to build on existing technologies; other projects may require advanced research and education to complete. Ultimately, the networking and technology infrastructure should be owned and managed by members of the Tulalip Tribes, with continuing partnerships among faculty and students from regional educational institutions.

We believe that the appropriate and selective use of technology will enhance the ability to respond to many of the education, community, cultural-preservation, business-development, and government needs of the Tulalip Tribes. Implemented incorrectly, technology will only serve as a source of frustration and high costs. The goal, however, is to truly understand the needs of end users, and then, only where appropriate, provide technical solutions that will help people reach their goals. This can only be achieved via an onsite presence.

Our Philosophy: Knowledge is the Key

In a world crowded with many technical solutions, it is easy to choose one that does not truly meet needs. Many technical projects result in extreme cost overruns, delayed implementations, minimal benefits, dismayed users and, unfortunately, lost opportunities. Corporate leaders and technology managers are often too quick to spend their money on tangible capital expenditures, such as computer hardware, peripherals, and networking solutions, without examining the true process and cultural needs of the organization. All too often, vendors and consultants encourage early spending, only to leave their clients with systems that are expensive or difficult to maintain. These cost overruns are directly attributable to lack of interest in the big picture beyond technology, or to lack of knowledge about the long-term cultural and organizational needs of the client.

Our approach is much different. The Tulalip Tribes leadership has endorsed the opportunity to build a partnership that has a foundation based on education and cultural understanding. Our team consists of college students, faculty, college administrators, tribal employees, and tribal executives. All members are motivated by an inherent interest in learning, interdisciplinary research, computer science, and long-term commitment to the needs of tribal members.

This special partnership is focused on determining the core infrastructure requirements. When time is taken to understand the requirements, the ability to implement the right solutions increases dramatically. Our approach includes several other distinguishing characteristics, listed below.

Ensure an unbiased and fair analysis.

Because the TTL team has no specific hardware, software, or client services to sell, our findings fairly represent the internal technology needs of the tribes. Also, students typically perform their best when given the opportunity to put theory into action.

Use effective systems analysis and computer science methods.

The faculty, staff, and student teams used many of the latest techniques in systems analysis and design, enhancing both the educational experience and technical benefits of the research.

Focus on identifying similar and specific needs of the various tribal organizations.

One of the project goals was to determine where organizations might be able to leverage shared data needs, thus reducing the amount of rework, minimizing data inaccuracies, and providing the ability to share information between different organizations and functions.

Demonstrate the long-term commitment to our community.

The TTL partnership is being designed for the long run, with a total commitment to the long-term future of the Tulalip Tribes, our students, and the education community. Students gain a rich understanding of the Tulalip Tribes' customs and culture–invaluable as they continue their work on real-world technology projects.

Complete the project with minimal cost and schedule overruns.

Instead of using high-priced consulting firms, students and tribal members will complete and manage the projects. The educational experiences are invaluable, and the interest in the success of the project is long-term. Future employment opportunities also exist for the participants.

Provide a strategy that will develop job opportunities and technology training for tribal members.

The implementation and management of technology will provide increased opportunities for employment as well as training for existing and new employees. Extensive education and hands-on training provide practical, real-world experiences that will capture the imagination and interests of all involved. Project teams that consist of students, faculty, tribal employees, and end users will be both enriching and fun.

Some Important First Steps

To have a chance of completing this project, we found it necessary to develop a core infrastructure and achieve some short-term successes. These core accomplishments set the stage for additional funding and project opportunities:

- Established operating agreement between The Tulalip Tribes, Everett Community College, and members of the University of Washington, Bothel
- Hired faculty consultants, support staff, and part-time student workers

- Provided cultural information and education to faculty, staff, and students about the tribes prior to working on their course and internship projects
- Configured computers, printers, network, and Internet server for the TTL Coordinating Center located in the Tulalip Education Center
- Developed TTL document management system to store, manage, and retrieve all technical documents
- Managed 23 student group projects (a total of 113 students), one internship, one research project, four UWB volunteers, and two Everett Community College volunteers
- Completed baseline hardware, software, and networking asset survey for existing tribal facilities, including floor plans
- Provided technical hardware guidance and implementation strategy for Computer in Every Tribal Member Home project
- Established relationship with principal representatives of the Tulalip Tribes
- Coordinated joint-venture opportunities with industry vendors regarding networking, telecommunications, hardware, and software requirements
- Identified and collected over 1,200 data forms used throughout the Tulalip Reservation
- Built a data dictionary including identification and consolidation of classes and attributes of approximately 90 percent of data currently collected on the reservation
- Generated over 6,000 pages of technical documentation and specifications to be used during the implementation phase
- Developed crucial relationships with tribal members who will provide guidance and support for implementation of new technologies
- Identified core pilot projects that will demonstrate the appropriate implementation of technology infrastructure

Implement Core Infrastructure Projects

While much work was completed in establishing the operational infrastructure, the bottom line is application. The identification of core tribal infrastructure projects was based on several criteria: providing access to computer hardware and software; developing a high-speed networking infrastructure; creating access to technical support; building communication via the Internet; creating jobs; and service learning. A geographic information system for land use and natural-resource planning, cultural and language preservation, business development, finance and human-resource management, tribal document management, website development, case management, online medical information systems, and a 911 dispatch center are currently being developed. These critical and highly visible projects will serve as a foundation for the future of the Tulalip Tribes.

Strategies for Effective Technology Implementation in Tribal Communities

The Tulalip Technology Leap initiative continues to make progress on many fronts. As with any organization, we face daily challenges and make some mistakes. What is most appreciated by all the staff and students is that each of the mistakes is converted into a learning opportunity for the future. Through weekly meetings and publishing of project schedules and timelines, students share and discuss challenges and approaches that work, and some that don't. The faculty and staff members have found this environment to be a model for learning, truly service learning at its best.

The following summary of strategies that have emerged from this project may be useful in other settings. Some may appear obvious, but the challenge is in the implementation.

Strategy 1: Achieve leadership through partnering. Charismatic leadership treats each team member as an individual, and providing intellectual growth opportunities is critical in a partnership of this type. Sincere participation in the concept and establishment of the community vision is essential. It is also important for each entity in the partnership to have attainable goals that meet the organizational goals of each partner institution.

Strategy 2: Create service-learning opportunities for both tribal and nontribal students. Service learning is increasing in importance at all levels of higher education. Perhaps one of the best strategies to span the Digital Divide is to encourage learning by doing, assuming access to technology. To offer tribal members technology courses with no opportunities to use the skills in the real world is an ineffective approach. Creating the opportunity for mentoring between the tribal members and two- and four-year students is invaluable. Students teach each other about technical theory and application concepts within the context of a particular culture.

Strategy 3: Understand the culture. To fully understand a culture requires getting beyond the external, visible symbols and progressing toward understanding the core values. Understanding the history, founders, cultural rites, and ceremonies is only one path to achieving that goal. This information appears to be best gained through immersion in the culture. In our project, we encourage students to participate in such diverse events as surveying the shellfish population or attending the closing ceremonies of a language camp for tribal children. Students have had the opportunity to learn about the relational nature of the tribes, distinctive from that of traditional corporate America.

Strategy 4: Ensure that technology is appropriate for the process. Successful technology implementation requires a firm understanding of the desired process. It is often easy to automate an existing process without changing it; the result can be frustration and resistance to future attempts to apply technology. Using effective listening and systems-analysis skills, students have identified ways to implement technology where appropriate. Perhaps more important is the fact that students develop a personal relationship and mutual trust that ultimately benefits everyone.

Strategy 5: Demonstrate short-term success within a long-term strategy. The vital idea is the concept of *show me.* Native-American history provides many examples of failed promises and lack of long-term commitment; this perception is easily generalized, and often warranted, as applied to the promises of technology. It is in the best interest of all to identify and complete projects that work. Building on a series of small, successful projects is an effective method of changing beliefs and overall attitude toward the larger technology strategy.

Strategy 6: Identify and educate future leaders. While finding effective leaders to start an ambitious project is challenging, a more difficult and often overlooked strategy is identifying and educating the leaders of the future. Ultimate tribal management of the technology infrastructure is critical, and new generations of leaders are essential. Designing effective K-12 programs, job training for young adults, and internship opportunities that are interesting and valuable are but a few of the steps that need to be taken immediately. Identification of tribal role models who share their own passion and excitement is critical.

Strategy 7: Disseminate project information. Often the fundamental concept of project visibility is the hardest to grasp. Part of building end-user trust and developer accountability is informing people of the true progress of projects. Web-based project management, newsletters, tribal newspapers, local and regional news coverage, and even national publications and conferences help inspire completion of projects. Continued communication between the developers, leaders, and tribal members is paramount. The effort spent on a project's visibility is often the principal factor in the project's success.

Strategy 8: Establish core metrics. As with any modern quality management approach, effective metrics are essential. An established method for identifying the appropriate metrics should be identified and supported by the leaders. Examples of metrics include network bandwidth use, database quality, number of education courses completed by tribal members, end-user requests for help, or general attitude surveys regarding changes in tribal processes. It is important that resources are allocated to collect and aggregate these metrics for appropriate decision making.

Ongoing Partnership

A project of this scope, nature, and significance has truly been a learning opportunity for all. While it is impossible to cite all of the learning situations that have occurred so far during this project, it is safe to say that there were many opportunities to examine our own thoughts and perceptions as we mixed technology with culture. There are also many general technical benefits that will enable the Tulalip Tribes to access technology through a high-speed network, dramatically increase literacy through training, and provide information services essential to members.

Finally, the TTL team could not have reached its current level of success without the help of the many members of the Tulalip Tribes who have generously provided information, ideas, guidance, support, and time to the students and staff of the TTL team. The tribe members' efforts have been crucial in building this foundation for the future of the many organizations, members of the Tulalip Tribes, and our region. We look forward to our ongoing partnership as we continue the implementation phase of this important initiative.

CHAPTER 8

TUNNELING THROUGH THE CYBERPIPES: WOMEN IN TECHNOLOGY IN THE COMMUNITY COLLEGE

Stella Perez, Cindy Miles, and Cynthia Wilson

When *Yahoo! Internet Live*, one of today's most popular technology magazines, released its 5th Anniversary Issue in September 2001, features included the 80 Most Popular Websites, 30 Greatest Net Events, and 17 People (and one sock puppet) Who Shaped the Net. Of the 17 people who shaped the Internet, four are women–a 30 percent female representation that at first glance appears positive. But closer scrutiny reveals that the women listed alongside such technology kings as Bill Gates, Steve Case, Al Gore, and Jeff Bezos represent a very different branch of techno-royalty. Cindy Margolis earned her place on the list as the most downloaded swimsuit pin-up on the Internet, and Pamela Anderson made the list because of her unsuccessful attempt to bar from Web distribution a homemade sex video she filmed with rock star Tommy Lee. Hilary Rosen, CEO of the Recording Industry Association of America and "forever remembered and perhaps reviled as the person who took down Napster" is there, as is Meg Whitman, President and CEO of eBay, an Internet phenomenon that was launched as a place to trade antiques and collectibles.

Critical examination of this list could lead to the conclusion that the women involved in today's hottest technology, the Internet, are litigious to a fault, engrossed in shopping to the point of livelihood, or fodder for the sex appeal of swimsuit calendars and tabloid headlines. It seems apparent that the criteria for selection to the list differ along gender lines; indeed, the list's celebration of female contributions to the Internet does little to advance the legacy of women in the field.

For more than a century, women have had a prominent place in the history of technology. Ada Byron King (1815-1852), who contributed to the vision and development of Babbage's computing machine, is the namesake for ADA, the first computer program which used a complex, block-structured language aimed at embedded applications. Evelyn Boyd Granville (1918-1985), the first African-American woman to earn a Ph.D. in mathematics (Yale), developed the computer programs that were used for trajectory analysis in the Mercury Project, the first U.S. manned mission in space, and the Apollo Project, which sent astronauts to the Moon. Joan Margaret Winters (1916-1998) was instrumental in the development of FORTRAN (Formula Translation) and was active in SHARE, an International Business Machines (IBM) computer user group. In 1976, at age 60, she joined SHARE's Human Factors Project, a group dedicated to educating IBM employees and clients about the importance of human factors in the design of computer hardware and software that led to much of the human and computer interface we use today.

One of the most legendary women in technology, Rear Admiral Grace Murray Hopper (1906-1992), graduated Phi Beta Kappa from Vassar College and then earned an M.A. in math and physics in 1930 and a Ph.D. in mathematics in 1934. After teaching at Vassar, she joined the Navy Reserve, despite perceptions that she was too old (34) and too light (105 pounds). This new path brought Hopper to four decades of pioneering work and the development of COBOL (Computer Object Business Operating Language), one of the most widely used computer languages ever created. Hopper's tenacity and leadership skills led her to a lifetime of outstanding contributions in academia, industry, the military, and computer science. In 1969, she was the first woman awarded the suddenly inappropriately named Computer Science Man-of-the-Year Award from the Data Processing Management Association. In 1973, she became the first person from the United States and the first woman of any nationality to be made a Distinguished Fellow of the British Computer Society. Her early recognition of the potential for commercial applications of computers and her leadership in making this vision a reality paved the way for modern data processing.[1]

---

[1] For more information about women in technology, see Grace Hopper Organization (www.gracehopper.org), Computer Research Association Committee on the Status of Women in Computing Research (www.cra.org), Institute of Women in Technology (www.iwt.org), MentorNet (www.mentornet.net), and Association for Computing Machinery Committee on Women in Computing (www.acm-w.org).

More recently, the first webmaster, librarian Louise Addis of the Stanford Linear Accelerator Center (SLAC), brought together a team that developed the first website in the United States. Launched in December 1991, it was considered a "revolutionary advance in technology [that] was the 'killer app' for the fledgling World Wide Web" (Trimm, 2001, p. 1). Still, the contributions of these and other pioneering women notwithstanding, technology fields remain dominated by men. A 2001 report by the National Council for Research on Women, *Balancing the Equation: Where Are Women and Girls in Science, Engineering and Technology?* (Thom, 2001) prompts questions as provocative as the one in its title: Why, since 45 percent of the U.S. workforce is female, do women hold only 12 percent of science and engineering jobs in business and industry? Why, since women have been earning more than 25 percent of the doctorates in science for over 30 years, do they hold less than 10 percent of the full professorships in the sciences, with "only 14 to 16 percent of the doctoral degrees awarded in computer science going to women" (Camp, 2001, p. 24)? This reality may help explain why the number of women seeking computer science degrees is declining; indeed, "even though 37.1 percent of computer science degrees were awarded to female students in 1984, only 26.7 percent of those degrees were awarded to women in 1998, a decrease of 28 percent" (Camp, 2001, p. 24).

The dearth of women in technology is reflected in our schools, our homes, and our offices, clear evidence that rifts in the Digital Divide include not only issues of racial, ethnic, and economic access, but of gender access as well. Expanding the conversation about technology access and opportunity to include an underrepresented group that by itself makes up over half the nation's population reveals that the goal of Digital Democracy is far from being achieved.

Clogs, Leaks, and Breaks in the Pipeline

The leaky pipeline is a concept that has been used to refer to the steady attrition of girls and women throughout the formal Science, Engineering, and Technology (SET) system, from primary education to SET careers and policy decision making.

The Congressional Commission on the Advancement of Women and Minorities in Science, Engineering, and Technology Development (July 2000) report, *Land of Plenty: Diversity as America's Competitive Edge in Science, Engineering and Technology*, points out that, "more than ever before, the ticket to a skilled job is a degree from an institution of higher education. However, while college enrollment is growing overall, the number of students who embark on SET majors is declining. And women, underrepresented minorities, and persons with disabilities–the smallest part of this shrinking pool of potential skilled labor–continue to face barriers including low expectations of academic potential, lack of finances, and inadequate precollege educational opportunities" (p. 4).

Female involvement in technology can be described as existing on a continuum that spans from childhood enthusiasm to adolescent disenchantment to adult rejection of technology as a career choice. The reduction in the number of women earning degrees in technology follows a clearly definable path, with high involvement in elementary grades steadily declining to a much lower interest by graduate school. Treu (qtd. in Holzberg, 1997, par. 2) describes a pipeline effect in computer science:

> There's no difference in the performance of young girls and boys in computer-related classes at the elementary school level. Both show a high degree of interest. Yet at every stage in the educational process, we lose more of the girls. In high school, fewer girls participate in computing activities such as programming contests. In college, women are less likely than men to major in computer science. Even fewer women go on to graduate school in these areas or seek computer-related academic and industrial research positions when they look for jobs.

Pointing out that leaks in the pipeline have caused "the steady attrition of girls and women throughout the formal S&T [science and technology] system, from primary education to S&T decision making," Sophia Huyer (2002), Executive Director of the Gender Advisory Board of the United Nations Commission on Science and Technology for Development, reports, "Women are underrepresented at every level of science and technology. They are undereducated, have fewer credentials, and are underemployed and clearly underpromoted around the world" (AAUW, par. 1). Huyer identifies five barriers to female participation in science and technology: "sociocultural attitudes, education, academic appointments, science and technology professions, S&T development and transfer" (AAUW, par. 1).

The scarcity of women in technology is not, at least initially, caused by a lack of interest. Girls are engaged at young ages, but their interest wanes early, in large part because childhood games are often designed for the male audience. The male-centered school curriculum does little to encourage girls, and as adults, women are faced with jobs designed for the male technology specialist. Brunner and Bennett (1998) explored this disparity and found that "the expert men and women in [the] sample had very different expectations of and feelings about technology" (par. 3). This difference was so distinct that they describe it as "a feminine and masculine 'voice' in the technological universe" (Brunner & Bennett, 1998, par. 3). Explaining these two voices, they note:

> The feminine attitude toward technology looks right through the machine to its social function, while the masculine view is more focused on the machine itself. One implication of this difference might be that presenting technology as an end in itself–a special subject of study (as in a programming class)–is less likely to appeal to young women than to young men. If the technology is introduced as a means to an end, such as a tool for in-depth research or for making a multimedia presentation, young women are as likely to find it appealing as young men. (Brunner & Bennett, 1998, par. 7)

Camp (2001) also reports this distinction, noting that, "While men usually focus on the computer and its technology, women most often focus on what the computer can do for society" (p. 24).

Technology and the Female Student

Although women generally have little enticement to enter technology fields, some do seek degrees and jobs in these areas. As with science, math, and engineering, though, "women are less likely than men" to select technology as a major field of study (*Land of Plenty*, 2000, p. 4).

This factor becomes more striking considered next to statistics indicating that, despite dramatic increases in enrollments for computer science degrees, "the percentage of women opting for IT careers is dropping fast" (Radcliff, 1999, par. 1). The American Association of University Women website (2000) reports, "Women receive less than 28 percent of the computer science bachelor's degrees, down from a high of 37 percent in 1984. Computer science is the only field in which women's participation has actually decreased over time" (www.aauw.org/2000/techsavvybd/html).

Not only are women not enrolling in these programs at the rate men are, but they are also dropping out of these programs at a greater rate than men, even when the women have higher grades than the men do. The women who earn degrees in computer technology "are usually the students who earn high grades," and although "many males with average grades earn [computer science] degrees.... very few females with average grades earn computing degrees" (Camp, 2001, p. 26). Camp explains that strong female students are more confident in their ability to succeed in a male-dominated field than are average students, whose feelings of inadequacy are reinforced in these programs.

This is particularly evident when computer science programs are housed in math, science, and engineering departments, which are traditionally unwelcoming to women. Camp (2000) reports that statistically, "women are less likely to obtain a degree from a computing department that is within an engineering college than from one in a non-engineering college, such as the College of Arts and Sciences" (p. 26). The study revealed that a computing department that moves from a non-engineering college to an engineering college "can expect an 18 to 26 percent decrease in bachelor's and master's degrees awarded to women and a 7 to 8 percent decrease in doctoral degrees awarded to women in their department" (p. 26).

Explanation rests partly in the strongly male computer culture. Sherry Turkle, Co-Chair of the American Association of University Women Education Foundation Commission on Technology, Gender, and Teacher Education, notes that the Commission's *Tech-Savvy* report "makes it clear that girls are critical of the computer culture, not computer phobic. Instead of trying to make girls fit into the existing computer culture, the computer culture must become more inviting for girls" (www.aauw.org/2000/techsavvybd.html).

Caught in the Pipeline: Women in IT Careers

Given the paucity of women entering technology programs, Radcliff's (1999, Abstract) report that, according to the U.S. Bureau of Labor Statistics, "the percentage of technical jobs held by women reportedly hangs at a static 28 percent, even as the number of women in the workforce approaches 50 percent" is not surprising. This phenomenon is explained in part by the *Land of Plenty* (2000) report:

> Despite decades of social change, the general perception remains that technical workers, scientists, and engineers are unusually intelligent White men who are socially inept, absent-minded nerds.... Such images discourage many underrepresented minorities, persons with disabilities, and especially women from pursuing any interest they may have in a SET career. (p. 7)

Women are also discouraged from entering computer technology fields because of an erroneous but persistent "stereotype that computing is a solitary and antisocial activity" (Camp, 2001, p. 26). They also have few role models to mentor, inspire, or otherwise encourage them to enter these professions.

Women, the Community College, and the IT Pipeline

The community college, long a champion of open access and equal opportunity, has among its students a large proportion of women; indeed, "women are more likely than men to attend community colleges" (MentorNet, 2001, p. 7). Community colleges are also engaged in preparing students for entry into or advancement in the workforce. With the large number of women enrolled in community colleges, these organizations seem ripe to support women pursuing technology fields. They may also seem the right places for women to be leaders in technology. Little specific data is available pertaining to the number of women in technology leadership positions in U.S. community colleges, making it necessary to rely instead on alternative sources such as CIO and other technology leadership listservs. A review of online activities and listservs indicates that few women hold these positions or, if they do, they do not engage in this kind of collegial interaction.

The numbers are surprisingly low, even among consortia as diverse as the League for Innovation in the Community College. The CIO Summit held annually at the League's *Conference on Information Technology* has a goal of creating a strong network of community college CIOs. The event is designed for technology leaders to explore issues, discuss strategies, review programs, and share creative approaches to information technology in the community college. In the three years of records available, participation of women at the CIO Summit dropped; in 1999, 10 of 53 participants were women (20 percent); in 2000, although the total number of participants increased (68), fewer of the participants were female (eight participants, or 12 percent). The decreasing percentage of female participants continued in 2001, when the CIO Summit had only 10 percent female representation (four of 41 participants).

The trend that favors male participation extends to the Summit's presenters as well. In 1999 and 2000, all panelists were male CIOs; in 2001, the panel included four male CIOs and one female CIO. In the 2002 Summit, two male CIOs and one female CIO participated on the panel. Although female participation is dropping, the CIO Summit is trying to be more inclusive by adding female CIOs to the panel.

In 2001, the researchers found so few women technology leaders in community colleges that they used snowballing to identify five female leaders–four in community colleges and one in a higher education organization–to participate in research. They developed an interview protocol that includes a mix of individual questions, grouped questions, and open-ended information requests. The researchers conducted initial interviews via e-mail, and follow-up questions and discussions were held via e-mail and telephone. The details and expression found in the completed surveys offered more than responses; the participants shared personal stories and histories of career choices, successes, and challenges in the technology field. These questions and the participant responses were reviewed through inductive analysis and organized by pattern-coded responses. The response patterns are organized below by question.

Describe your management style. How do you develop processes?

The CIO leaders used words such as "participatory," "consultative," "empowering," "inventive," "spontaneous," "collaborative," and "mentoring" to describe their management style, words that to some extent mirror the attributes of women's engagement in technology described in the literature (Bennett & Bruner, 1998; Camp, 2001). Researchers were also struck by the unassuming tone of their comments, exemplified here by one respondent who noted the push and pull of leadership, organization, people, and motivation:

> A self-description of my management style isn't very accurate. We all want to say that we're participatory, collaborative, nurturing, creative, etc. Sometimes I am all of those things; sometimes I'm not. I push myself and my organization to set and meet high standards of delivery. I like to work with staff who value a wide-open discussion of how best to achieve our objectives. With the right mix of personalities and skill sets, this is a lot of fun.

Corresponding with the collective management styles of respondents, their organizational processes and decisions are made with "focus and understanding of the big picture," "through recognition of shared space," by "first creating a communication strategy," and with "senior members of the team actively participating in the development of processes." Another comment underscored the level of input in process development cycles focused on refinement and recognition of improvement for next opportunities: "Once the project is complete, we reassemble for a quick recap and share observations that should improve the process for next time."

What brought you into IT? Why have you chosen to stay in IT?

Recognizing the challenging pathway for women in IT careers, researchers asked the five technology leaders to describe the reasons they became IT professionals and why they have remained in these careers despite the obstacles to advancement. In their responses, the women also outlined the routes they took to become IT leaders. All five started in math, science, computer science, or business fields and knew that their career plans were nontraditional and risky. Only one of the five sought a career in education, and that career led her to technology:

> At the time I was in school, my goal was to be a mathematics teacher, but IT work chose me. Being in education, there weren't funds to contract IT services so I volunteered or agreed when asked to take on IT projects.

Another IT leader entered education as a second career and came to technology through professional development as she "looked for ways to improve and enhance [her] teaching skills." She saw that "technology tools showed tremendous potential for instruction."

Two of the women were not interested in following the more traditional path of degreed women in their era. One explained, "With degrees in math and no interest in teaching, I went to work for a major research laboratory." Her entry into an IT career was not planned; she learned to program in her job at the laboratory and, as she put it, "One step led to another and, over time, I moved through various technical positions, then into management. I did not make a conscious choice of IT as a career field." Another respondent had a more strategic reason for entering the IT field by selecting computer programming as a minor to her math major. She explained that she "chose this career, frankly, because in 1970 it was one of the best paying careers for women."

These women chose to stay in IT careers for many of the same reasons that they first chose nontraditional fields of study. They described the work as "challenging" and "ever-changing." One expressed satisfaction in "being part of the frontier spirit" that characterizes the IT world. Despite the barriers and relatively small representation of women in technology, they also described the IT field as providing "more opportunities" for them.

Describe your greatest obstacles and challenges. How have you addressed or overcome them?

The obstacles and challenges these women identified fall into three categories: access, accountability, and perceived value. Respondents offered few specific examples of how they have overcome the obstacles and challenges they identified; instead, most noted that they work toward stronger relationships, better communication strategies, and targeted outcomes to address issues of access, accountability, and perceived value.

Access. These leaders identified access to technology as among the greatest obstacles, primarily for the students they serve. One described her college's agricultural service area, which has one of the lowest per capita income rates in the state, as one in which many of the students "do not have technology available in their homes." She explained the college's responsibility for providing technology access in this community, noting that the "limited access and availability of technology in students' homes … requires a substantial amount of available [technology] resources accessible to students on campus." She argued that the college needs current technology to "prepare students to meet the needs of a technological society," an argument strengthened by the community's perception of the college as "a real source of hope" for improving the area's standard of living.

Another leader shared concerns of access to technology tools and applications as a perpetual obstacle to the growth and development of females leading technological initiatives:

> Those of us in education have all heard of or know firsthand the growing gap between those with technology skills and those without. As administrators and leaders, we are struggling to justify what we are doing with technology and keeping up with innovation rather than focusing on training and building bridges for those who have had limited or no access to technology tools. We act as though those who are not active in technology fields have all done this by choice rather than resignation.

Accountability. Responses from the technology leaders indicated their recognition of the need to communicate the benefits of technology investments to students, staff, and administrators and to establish accountability measures and performance indicators to help ensure that these benefits are fully realized. One respondent described the need to "show ways that [technology] makes our college community's job easier" and "to ensure the technology is used responsibly and within the guidelines provided by the state system." Another argued that technology is a permanent fixture in our lives and work places, so a different approach to accountability is needed: "We are struggling to justify what we are doing as though there is a choice about whether or not to move ahead. We can choose which technologies, but we can't turn back time."

A third respondent provided a rich account of challenges posed by technology investment issues, notably including the importance of building relationships in dealing with these challenges:

> One of the key challenges of my career, and I think of IT in general, is the difficulty of making the case of the value, the [return on investment] for the application of information technology in new, creative, and extended directions. Until the last few years the general sense was that IT was an expense, and needed to be viewed from a cost-control perspective. Over time that has changed; most institutions recognize the critical value of information technology, that real transformation of processes cannot be effected without technology, and that basic competitive positioning is dependent on technology. I have tried to develop an approach to communication with upper management and governing boards regarding these issues that emphasizes the resulting value of the application of technology. I strive to find the extent of technical detail that is relevant to the audience, address alternatives from functional and cost perspectives, and make a business case that the direction and outcomes justify the expense. Establishing a relationship with upper management and the governing board is essential to serving the institution well with respect to technology investments.

Perceived Value. In the midst of shrinking budgets and growing technology expenses, the perceived value of technology is a significant obstacle to the development and penetration of technological innovations. Although learning and teaching should be the service priorities, convincing others that the expense of technology tools is a direct support of those processes is difficult. One respondent described her quest for support:

> As the major sales manager for technology, I have to apply the skills of a magician and the wisdom of a futurist to ask for the essential dollars to support technology. Many times these dollars aren't real visible to the other administrators competing for these same dollars. The dollars related to technology might be copper to support more telephone lines or switches to increase speed. To convince the competitors of the need for these dollars, it is essential to show them what we will lose without this needed technology.

Another respondent described "perception, education, and training" of colleagues and others regarding the value of technology as the greatest challenges. Admitting that "technology is expensive," she explained that "many perceive that money spent to keep technology current is taking money away from other programs. It is a challenge to explain, to the satisfaction of skeptics, the justification of technology as a priority."

Only one respondent specifically identified a gender issue as a significant challenge to her work and role:

> With all of the challenges of availability and accessibility of technology, it is essential to be a wise shopper. Many times the 'snow application' will be applied. Especially as a woman IT executive, I have found male sales individuals to want to apply the tactics of 'you really don't understand the technology so get me a male staff member who knows what they are doing.'

Other women in the interview group did not specify gender as contributing to the obstacles and challenges they face in their work. Their responses focused instead on access, accountability, and perceived value.

What do you believe are the greatest future obstacles or challenges in the IT world?

The five technology leaders recognized people, progress, and the unknown as the three most distinct obstacles or challenges in the future. With regard to people and progress, they acknowledged that great efforts will be necessary to maintain a steady flow of well-trained, competent staff to develop and implement new technology-based initiatives. Leadership, along with a grasp of new dimensions and new phases, will be critical to making good use of technological innovations. One respondent focused particularly on leadership and staff recruitment and development:

> Those of us who serve as leaders in IT want to be on the cutting edge with technology, but not the bleeding edge. We need to choose wisely in the selection of staff members, those individuals who are willing to grow and change with the constant demands. With a continual stream of new technologies, a great deal of time will be spent researching, applying, and defending the most appropriate technologies.

Again reflecting findings in studies by Bennett and Bruner (1998) and Camp (2001), one respondent described the challenge of focusing on "what we can achieve with technology as the tool" to better "facilitate the successful and consistent use" of the technology. One respondent was specific in identifying current challenges, mentioning difficulties associated with several factors:

> privacy, in particular related to personal information but also the ethical and legal use of company information; reliability of the Internet for business transactions. . . recruitment, retention, and training of staff; and the search for the balance point between costs and benefits of the deployment of technology are key challenges.

Along with the tangible challenges, these women also recognized the unanticipated, unexpected, and unknown aspects that characterize the technological future. One respondent emphasized that "adjusting all of our thinking to work in a world where change and development happen faster and faster will stretch our flexibility and challenge us in ways we haven't experienced." Similarly, another respondent spoke of the greatest challenge as "the one that sneaks up on us." One technology leader discussed the "personal challenge" of her diminishing "grasp of the details of technology" as her responsibilities increase. She remarked that "integration of telephone, computers (large, small, and in between), Web services, and now broadcasting make every IT director's life a continual leap into the unknown."

One respondent moved beyond the immediate scope of her particular position, confronting the limitations of provincial perspectives with the realities of greater human challenges:

> People believe technology and computer access will be ubiquitous soon, not realizing that food is not even ubiquitous yet. Electricity, water, all the resources we take for granted are scarce in so much of the world. The gap between first and third world nations feels like it is growing.

From local challenges of staffing and professional development to broader concerns about the rapid pace of change in technology to recognition of the global impact of technology in a world still characterized by subsistence economies, these women expressed a need for IT professionals to be prepared for whatever the future brings. Their focus on building relationships and practical applications of technology also supported the findings in the literature.

What are your greatest successes?

In response to the question on success, two of the technology leaders described specific project and project leadership experiences, but, countering the stereotype of IT as a solitary profession, all respondents identified relationships with others, staff efforts, team development, collaboration, and creating opportunities for others as their greatest successes. For all respondents, success was not a solitary victory; instead, they listed the work of a supportive and engaged team as a major factor contributing to that success. For example, one CIO described the selection and implementation of an integrated administrative system in a limited timeframe as a project in which "many people gave a remarkable effort to ensure that we met the deadlines." Another hailed the "innovative and collaborative approaches which have stretched limited technology dollars and provided opportunities to students interested in technology careers."

One technology leader described a project in a former position as among her greatest successes, again emphasizing the collaborative nature of the project's success:

> In a previous position with a Fortune 50 high-tech corporation, I led a group of representatives from IT organizations across the corporation in the development of a data management architecture that was agreed to and implemented. The group brought together engineers with specific technical expertise, analysts with business perspective, programmers, IT managers, all with a view as to the desired outcome. My role was to lead this disparate group to a common architecture, facilitating the path to resolution and agreement, and then to an implementation strategy. The resulting outcome was years ahead of the work in other companies and the industry in general.

Others described their successes as the people for whom they have served as mentors. One mentor noted that "watching the development of some of these folks provides the most satisfaction," while another remarked that "helping staff members use technology to…. achieve their job duties and find the power available to them using technology" is a great success.

Not all discussion of greatest successes centered on collaboration, however, and two examples particularly suggest the pride these women take in bringing an idea to life. One technology leader said,

> Making it happen best reflects my greatest successes. On several occasions, I have been given a vague concept or idea to develop and implement. I've continued to work to expand and grow the availability of technology in education where I have worked.

Another remembered an experience in an earlier job:

> In a previous position, I started with empty space and a budget. From that, I developed and implemented the educational computing program for a 7,000-FTE-student junior college.

To what do you attribute your success?

Most of these technology leaders attributed their success to hard work and, as they did in identifying their greatest successes, all respondents noted the contributions of others. One pointed to the "smart, dedicated people" she has worked with throughout her career as "the key ingredient for any success" she has had. Another credited "supportive administrations that are forward-thinking in addressing technology needs in education and who remain focused on student success." Another said she focuses "on the human side of the process, the people, how the technology impacts what they are trying to achieve," noting also that she "like[s] to support the success of others." Another approached the contributions of others in a different way–learning from them–by pointing out the importance of "asking good questions" and "not being afraid of saying, 'I don't know, teach me.'"

Who are your role models?

Researchers asked the IT leaders who their role models were, and the lack of female role models in IT is reflected in their responses. For these leaders, role models come from their families, from colleagues outside the IT area, and from composites of people and events in their lives. Of family, one technology leader credited her parents for providing "the model to believe I could do anything I set my mind to do . . . [and] the road to getting anything was hard work, perseverance, and standing behind the product." Another women cited her husband and his "skills in wending a way through complicated people issues with humor, compassion, and a focus on results that benefit the organization and all the individuals involved."

The women technology leaders also described their colleagues as role models. One reported that her president "has encouraged me in the pursuit of technology for our college" and supports the role of technology in instruction and administrative services by providing "the resources needed to make technology happen at our college." Another spoke of her colleagues more generally:

> I look to people who have been on my staff. I've admired one's technical competence, another's choices on life balance, and another's ability to rally a team to extraordinary accomplishment. They have been models for me, too.

Another respondent spoke of balance, but in reference to her *tai chi* teacher, a former high-tech executive who now "demonstrates and reminds me that *tai chi* is not performance sport, we are going nowhere, and we will never get there. The moment of moving meditation is what matters."

Other respondents referred to different kinds of role models. One mentioned that she didn't have any "complete role models." Instead, she had "valued characteristics from many people" and reminded herself that "a trait ... was admirable, and [she] should do [her] best to emulate it." Another described her role models as "people you've never heard of, women of earlier generations who were never limited by the society in which they lived–women who struggled for every opportunity." She cited specifically her mother, a friend of her mother's generation, and "current industry leaders like Marjorie Scardino, the President at Pearson, who has staked her professional reputation on her understanding that technology will have an impact on the future of that company, a huge risk for a woman who could have ridden on the successes she has already enjoyed."

One respondent noted the absence of female leadership and camaraderie in technology fields:

> I haven't had many role models in IT. I've often felt that I was plowing new ground. I have had the good fortune to work with supervisors who have encouraged my efforts and provided opportunities for me to advance in a field that had few women role models as I advanced.

The responses indicate that these women seek in their role models both professional guidance and life guidance, and that they find role models not only where they work, but also where they live. Absent female IT colleagues, these women have found mentors and role models, women as well as men, in non-technology colleagues, in their families and friends, and in other people with whom they interact. From these role models they have learned the value of hard work, tenacity, risk-taking, relationships, and pride in a job well done. They have taken these lessons to heart as they have pushed their way through the pipeline toward the cyberceiling.

Repairing the Pipes: Recommendations

Although progress for women in IT careers has been slow, the careers of the five women interviewed demonstrate that leaks in the pipeline can be plugged. The literature and the responses from the interview participants suggest three specific recommendations for increasing female participation in technology development, application, and instruction: (1) more women as role models, (2) professional development in teacher education, and (3) technology beyond the bits and bytes.

These recommendations led researchers to pose two follow-up questions to the participants as women leading technology initiatives in community colleges; four participants responded. The first question–*In what ways, if any, are you serving as a role model or mentor for female students enrolled in IT programs at your college?*–extended beyond the personal experience of having role models to the respondents themselves serving as role models for women in technology. The second question–*What recommendations would you have for community colleges to increase the participation and success of female students in IT programs?*–asked respondents to make specific recommendations for encouraging female enrollment in IT programs.

Women as Role Models

Of the four respondents, only two had direct contact with students regularly; however, all four identified their work with other professionals and their leadership of technology-based committees as part of their role-model and mentoring efforts. One technology leader described her position as a role model for female leadership: "I chair the technology steering committee, and I participate on subcommittees that establish visibility and leadership of technology across the college." Noting no formal or direct mentoring of students, one respondent claimed:

> I occasionally have students as temp workers in our area and bring them into the life of the department. During this time, they see 50 percent of our IT management staff as women, and the top manager is also female. I hope that the presence of senior women in IT serves as an inspiration.

Although many indications point to mentoring as a positive impact point, one female technology leader who does have regular and direct contact with student populations identified a lack of interest by female students in accepting the opportunity:

> I have been supervising the instructional area of Computer Networking in our CIT courses since January

2001. I do have student contact with those interested in the networking area and students already enrolled in computer courses. In the past, I have volunteered to mentor female students who were interested in IT fields; unfortunately, the mentoring group had no takers.

Respondents remarked that traditional student services, vocational programming, and workforce development opportunities can be targeted to influence women in technology. However, a common challenge with attracting females to college programs lies in the flexibility and scheduling of course offerings. A clear recommendation for mentoring is providing opportunities of multiple contact points, resource references, and flexible meeting options.

In addition to campus-based student service developments, online services and resources offer advantages and outreach opportunities as support systems and resources for women. The Association for Computing Machinery's Committee on Women in Computing (www.acm-w.org) works with college computing departments to organize ACM-W student chapters, which then engage in activities designed to recruit and retain women in computing fields (Camp, 2001, p. 24). Another organization, Systers.org, encourages women pursuing technology degrees to participate in online communities that support females in technology fields. Camp (2001) reports that the Systers online community "consists of more than 2,500 women computer scientists in 38 countries" and offers forums for female computing students, faculty, and doctoral candidates (p. 24).

Expanding beyond the outreach philosophy of mentoring, the literature reports K-12 support for targeting women in IT careers, and Butler (2000) notes that "sex differences in attitudes toward computers were strongly established by grade eight" and that "early adolescence is an important time to make a difference" (pars. 7, 8). One CIO shared an example of a reach-back opportunity to initiate interest at earlier stages and increase the participation and success of female students in IT programs at her college:

We are beginning efforts with our tech-prep and dual-credit staff to work with area high schools to inform and recruit students. This is another opportunity to attract young women to the IT offerings. This is a new effort for my area so we're in the infancy stage. We are also a regional academy for Cisco with high schools as local academies. Again, this is a good opportunity to work with secondary education to attract new students. We are still looking for ways to attract women who might not have considered IT as a possibility.

Professional Development in Teacher Education

Recommendations to employ and retain IT professionals in faculty and leadership roles and to enroll and hold on to students in IT career programs emphasize the need for recruitment and development of female faculty teaching IT courses. Camp (2001) reports that "a study by Hornig shows that same-sex role models provide strong positive effects; thus, it is incumbent upon universities to attract, retain, and encourage female students and faculty in computer sciences" (p. 24). Camp posits that hiring women faculty in computing departments is "the most important move a university can make" in providing role models, but acknowledges the difficulty of making this move since women earn no more than 14 to 16 percent of the doctoral degrees in computer science (p. 24).

Encouraging women to enter technology fields and become technology educators necessitates a strong teacher training program that emphasizes use of technology applications in the learning environment. A common current practice in this kind of training is a drive-by approach where the focus is on the technical properties of hardware with no emphasis on educational applications or innovative uses of computing for multiple subject areas. Studies that have indicated a strong difference between male and female approaches to technology (Brunner & Bennett, 1998; Camp, 2001) suggest that this practice is tailored for the male student group; female students, then, would be more fully engaged in the course or program if faculty included in the curriculum the specific application of technology to, for example, improve peoples' lives.

All interview respondents to the second follow-up question commented on the need for a more sensitive faculty who not only focus on the rote memory of programming code and routines, but also address more collaborative endeavors with technology applications. Camp (2001) shares this approach and notes, "To help counteract this stereotype [that computing is a solitary and antisocial activity], computer science faculty can adopt cooperative learning techniques in their classrooms, assign group problem-solving activities, and invite local industry employees (preferably women) to the campus to discuss a typical day at their job" (p. 26).

Technology Beyond the Bits and Bytes

The scarcity of women in IT leadership is not simply a matter of numbers; it is also a cultural issue. Looking beyond the binary code and hardware programming, one female CIO noted that as part of a guest lecture series she offers to students enrolled in one of the college technology programs, she addresses the realities of PC support. She talks broadly about the nontechnical skills necessary to support technology services, such as "confidentiality, communication skills, and patience." Some might not consider these traits as part of the application of technology, but they are critical skills that move more general users toward technical experience and expertise and influence the nature of the field through sociotechnical impact, or merging of technical and organizational change.

One respondent commented on the need and opportunity for women to explore more deeply their understanding of technological relationships and "applying concepts to higher education that require an understanding of . . . the technology, interpreting new trends, and thoughtful application in the organizational structure." Her comments are reflected in literature that underscores the need for diverse perceptions in the development of technology and its applications. At the 2001 Annual Meeting of the Association of American Colleges and Universities, Kennedy School Professor Jane Fountain emphasized the role of diversity in technology design and use, noting that,

> Important streams of research in psychology and management demonstrate that diversity in problem-

solving groups leads to different and often better outcomes. The results tend to be more inclusive, that is, they tend to take into consideration the values, interests, and needs of a variety of different parties. Attention to a wider range of computing users would benefit society. ("Jane Fountain," p. 20).

Although studies indicate that men and women approach technology differently, researchers recognize the value of these diverse perspectives in advancing the field. One author warns against a gender divide in technology: "The less considered danger of the gender gap concerns the advancement of the field as a whole. By hindering half of the population of potential contributors, the field of computer science decreases its chance of further development" ("Gender Gap," par. 4).

Responses to interview questions in the current study indicate that these women technology leaders in community colleges are aware of the need to open the pathway for other women. One mutually expressed theme among the interview respondents was the need to focus and use collective support to offset disparity:

> In the business environment women face many of the same challenges as in education. Glass ceilings exist, and we need to take a lesson from other parts of the industry where strong bonds of support, networking, and collaboration exist. In some fields, women have really banded together and made more inroads than I see in higher education.

The Past As Prologue

History provides ample evidence of many influential people who have shaped our lives and our societies, including the strong presence of women in the development of information technology. In a 2002 campaign soliciting support for the National Women's History Museum, Sally Ride, the first woman in space, wrote:

American women have been pioneers and partners in the fields of science, medicine, government, law, education, social service, literature, philanthropy, the arts, sports, business, and in the nurture of family and community from before our nation was founded until today. Ours is a wonderful legacy of accomplishment by extraordinary women. The stories of their lives should be known by all and taught to our children. Yet in one typical sixth-grade history book, only seven pages out of 631 are devoted to women. Less than 5 percent of our national and state monuments commemorate women. In other words, half of American history has never been told!

Moving from past to present, Butler (2000) offers a set of "computer equity themes" of the 1980s and 1990s that are still relevant today, including boys having a "more positive attitude toward computers" than girls, a "cultural bias that technology is a male domain," the "perception that computer technology is linked to mathematics, a field that girls feel is identified more with males," and "a lack of women as role models" (pars. 4, 5). At a time when popular images of women in technology do not often present this half of the population as serious partners in the IT world, educators must search the past, the present, and the future for ways to engage women seriously in technology fields.

As the open door to higher education, community colleges know well that as many as half of their students are traditionally underrepresented in science, engineering, and technology. They know, too, that equity in computer access, knowledge, and use cannot be measured solely by how many people use e-mail, surf the Net, or perform basic functions on the computer. The new benchmark for gender equity should emphasize computer fluency for women as well as men: not only the mastery of analytical skills and computer concepts, but also the ability to imagine innovative uses for technology across a range of problems and subjects. These sociotechnical values set a new standard for gender equity and emphasize new criteria of expertise.

REFERENCES

Allen, S. G. (2001, April). Technology and the Wage Structure. *Journal of Labor Economics, 19*(2), 440-483. Accessed via ProQuest, October 15, 2001.

American Association of University Women (AAUW). Review of *Tech-Savvy: Educating Girls in the New Computer Age.* www.aauw.org/2000/techsavvybd/html. Accessed November 5, 2001.

American Association of University Women Educational Foundation Commission on Technology, Gender, and Teacher Education. (2000). *Tech-Savvy: Educating Girls in the New Computer Age.* Washington, DC: Author.

Brown, B. L. (2001). Women and Minorities in High Tech Careers. *ERIC Digest* No. 226. ERIC Clearinghouse on Adult, Career, and Vocational Education.

Brunner, C., & Bennett, D. (1998, February). Technology Perceptions by Gender. *The Education Digest, 63*(6), 56-58. Accessed via ProQuest, October 9, 2001.

Butler, D. (2000, March/April). Gender, Girls, and Computer Technology: What's the status now? *The Clearing House, 73*(4), 225-229. Accessed via ProQuest, October 9, 2001.

Camp, T. Women in Computer Sciences: Reversing the Trend. *Syllabus*, August 2001, pp 24-26. www.syllabus.com/syllabusmagazine/article.asp?id=4576

Congressional Commission on the on the Advancement of Women and Minorities in Science, Engineering, and Technology Development (2000, July). *Land of Plenty: Diversity as America's Competitive Edge in Science, Engineering and Technology.* Summary of the Report. www.nsf.gov/od/cawmset/report.htm

The Gender Gap in the Computing Field, 1(1). (1998, March 16). www-cse.stanford.edu/classes/cs201/Projects/gender-gap-in-education/page6.htm. Accessed November 5, 2001.

Holzberg, C. S. (1997, May/June). A Gender-Equitable Classroom. *Technology and Learning, 17*(8), 42-23. Accessed via ProQuest, October 9, 2001.

Huyer, S. (2002, February 5). The Leaky Pipeline: Gender Barriers in Science, Engineering and Technology. *Gender and the Digital Divide Seminar Series #15.* www.workdbank.org/gender/ digitaldivide/ sophiahuyer.htm.

Jane Fountain on Women in the Information Age. (2001, Spring). *Liberal Education*, 20.

MentorNet Helps Women Students in Technical Careers. (2001, August). *Women in Higher Education*, 6-7.

Radcliff, D. (1999, January 18). Champions of Women in Technology. *Computerworld, 33*(3), 46-48. Abstract and full text. Accessed via ProQuest, October 9, 2001.

Thom, M.(2001). *Balancing the Equation: Where Are Women and Girls in Science, Engineering and Technology?* National Council for Research on Women. http://www.ncrw.org/research/iqsci.htm.

Trimm, M. (2001, December). From the President. *ACUTA News, 30*(12), 1.

Turkle, S. (2000). Review of *Tech-Savvy: Educating Girls in the New Computer Age.* (2000). American Association of University Women website. www.aauw.org/2000/techsavvybd.html. Accessed November 5, 2001.

CHAPTER 9

ON THE ROAD TO DOTCALM IN EDUCATION

Mark David Milliron

It just feels like we're moving too fast.

I have been a part of more than 200 campus visits, presentations, or workshops over the last five years, and the feedback from very thoughtful educators almost always includes this comment. And there's a reason for the feeling. In *The Innovator's Dilemma*, Christensen (1997) makes the powerful point that our society is experiencing the fastest adoption of a disruptive technology in human history. Industrial societies had anywhere from 20 to 50 years before disruptive innovations like electricity, automobiles, and televisions hit mass use (defined as 25 percent adoption) and drastically changed their work, play, and learning. Our information-age society, however, had little more than four years to adjust to the World Wide Web's move to mass use; we are only now beginning to arise after being digitally swept off our feet.

A useful image to put this challenge in context comes from modern Buddhist thinkers and practicing psychologists. Monks and therapists alike talk about the need to use meditation or other mindfulness techniques to slow ourselves down from our busy lives. In essence, we need to stop the car, take a deep breath, and metaphorically clean our windshields before we continue on the road ahead. Many, however, just keep speeding along. As they race ahead, they become less capable of making thoughtful choices about future directions, because as the daily grime and grit builds up, they lose sight of what's right in front of them. In extreme cases, some end up in painful personal and professional crashes.

While individual differences abound regarding the need for and value of different meditative or relaxation techniques, there is little doubt that many of us are only just getting our bearings after what felt like a ridiculous joyride over the last six years. It was a raucous race on the fledgling information superhighway, with our organizational cars full of folks intoxicated with what Allen Greenspan called "irrational exuberance." And, after the broader society's dotcom crash, it seems our collective motors are only now beginning to hum again. As this journey continues, the call comes again for us to examine both our direction and who will be included on the trip.

This book, *From Digital Divide to Digital Democracy*, has taken pains to outline significant trends and provide convincing data about our need to include all students in our journey down the road ahead. We've spent a good deal of time featuring model programs from educational institutions far and wide, showcasing leaders, teachers, and learners taking on this challenge. And as a final complement to these compelling profiles, I'd like to again sound a call for us all to commit not only to increasing the likelihood of digital inclusion, but to facilitating the underpinnings of Digital Democracy. I'd like to echo the hundreds of educators who have counseled caution for those still excited about the road ahead. In essence, they urge us to clean the windshield and keep our eyes open for a host of hazards.

Road Hazards

Looking for road hazards on a journey takes concentration. It's not often practiced by those with a need for speed or those caught up in their competitive drives. These folks tend to note hazards only after an accident. We want to be more thoughtful than that here, particularly with the hazards on the road ahead for education: hazards on the individual, organizational, and societal levels.

Individual Road Hazards

One of the most difficult individual road hazards to avoid is *the tendency to fake it—to act as though we understand the technology dialogue or infrastructure just so we don't appear to be behind the times.* I've been in meetings with college presidents, faculty members, student service leaders, and even chief information officers where serious faking is going on. I think we all have. People spew IT acronyms as though everyone understands them, and everyone in the room nods knowingly. I'm convinced I've been in technology-related discussions where at least three-quarters of the participants are completely lost, but for some reason we continue to blithely banter about the power of a new technology. Let's be honest: sometimes we just don't want to be the one who doesn't get it. I have to admit it: I've faked it. Have you?

We have to stop faking it. Put simply, faking it leads to tragic outcomes in education. Colleges have invested millions of dollars on vaporware systems because they were afraid of asking hard questions, not to mention their dread of the slings and arrows of being regarded as behind the times. To this day, I consider the "train is leaving the station, get on board or be left behind" rhetoric for adopting technology weak at best and frightening at worst. That others are doing it, or that we may be out of fashion, seems a dangerously sophomoric reason to spend enormous time and money on an initiative with such broad-ranging and possibly traumatic implications. We all can advance far more compelling reasons to adopt technology, many of which you've explored throughout this book.

We view true courage in action in our techno-enamored age when we see colleagues putting their egos on the line to say, "I have no idea what we're talking about." There is power in admitting ignorance. We may not ever want or need to develop a deep understanding of every detail, but we are more likely to understand the implications of IT decisions, not to mention more likely to learn. The good news is that information technology hardware and software change is so rapid that we are all novices every six months, so we always have kindred spirits. The best and the brightest in technology counsel us that we all have to be ready and willing to be rookies–often–to truly make IT work for us on the road ahead. Dangerous things can happen if we let our egos get in the way of honest IT dialogue and assessment.

Closely related to the faking-it phenomenon is the seduction of the new and novel. In a five-year international study of teaching-excellence-award winning faculty called *Practical Magic: On the Front Lines of*

Teaching Excellence, participants made the cogent observation that when it comes to technology and teaching and reaching students, we have to be sure not to use technology for the novelty, but the utility (Roueche, Milliron, & Roueche, 2003). This concern is real–as anyone who has suffered from a death-by-PowerPoint presentation can attest. For many of us, there is a time during a presentation when, as each slide swooshes across the screen in the pitch-black room and each major point screeches to a halt, bullet by bullet, we are only moments from a primal scream and a run for the door. Sandy Shugart, President of Valencia Community College (FL), is fond of noting that "all too often, PowerPoint presentations have neither power nor a point!"

This truism came crashing home for me in the mid-1990s. I adopted presentation graphics early and used them to jazz up my talks with as many new gimmicks as I could muster. I took pride in my new acumen and worked to make my presentations jump from the screen. But one day after a presentation about student motivation, during which I had tried to catalyze a dynamic dialogue on connecting with students, I was paid a compliment. An extremely kind woman said, "That was the best PowerPoint presentation I've ever seen." It hit me like punch in the chest. In that moment I realized that as my bells and whistles melodiously ring and blow, they run the risk of muting the message that matters. I immediately became a minimalist user of presentation graphics. I still use them; however, I'm constantly working to ensure that the few slides I use supplement rather than dominate the dialogue. Moreover, I'm more interested in making my presentation a resource *after* the engagement than a point of attention *during* it.

It comes down to the art of what some call making technology transparent. As Michael McGrath (2001) notes in his widely cited *Product Strategy for High Technology Companies*, all too often businesses are overly enamored with new technology, so much so that they actually frustrate customers and reduce profitability. For example, in *Loyalty.com: Customer Relationship Marketing in the Age of the Internet*, Newell and Rogers (2001) note that a primary reason people visit websites is to get a contact phone number. Yet many businesses are so eager to force customers to use the latest and greatest Web service that they bury their phone numbers four or five links deep on the site. The result is technology that is in the way, and customers who switch to more user-friendly companies. The faculty members in the *Practical Magic* study were quick to note that the corollary effect can easily happen in education–new technology can get in the way of learning. The class session goes off course and becomes a journey down Tech-Support Lane as the videodata projector refuses to work, or important class sessions screech to a halt as all are encouraged to share in the glory of a slide show that uses all the new features. Some teachers even make the unthinkingly benign but nonetheless powerfully symbolic mistake of literally turning their backs to their students as they read from the PowerPoint screen.

In a 1997 article titled *The Technology Prayers*, Cindy Miles and I closed with an earnest call: "Please make IT go away." It was a call for help to any higher power possible to make technology transparent, to help us transition to a time when we view the Internet and its associated technologies as we do electric lights or power outlets: simple utilities that we assume work. We were echoing the call from educators nationwide who long to be free to focus first on connecting with learners and connecting them to learning.

A closely related roadblock builds on the intoxication with the new and novel as it makes us more effective. As individuals surrounded by technology at every turn, *we are uniquely challenged to find the balance between multitasking and mindfulness*. There are education articles from the 1970s rife with predictions about the rise of information technology and robotics and how these trends were going to create a new challenge for education. Because of the number of jobs lost to technology and robotics, and the increase in wealth and leisure time, education would have to create more avocational programs to help people adjust to the new lifestyle. Of course, the opposite has happened. Economists now praise the rise in worker productivity brought on by technology (Greenspan, 2002). We now can produce more work per worker than we ever thought possible in the United States. Moreover, we take our work with us wherever we go. Our home computers are weekend work stations. Our cell phones have become constant companions as we strive to stay connected. And e-mail, the aptly named "killer application" of the

Internet, has moved from unique communication form to deadly burden. We now are urged to use Blackberry devices or buy Internet phones just so we can keep up. And, worst of all, some workers have become more and more like Pavlov's dogs: at the ding of incoming e-mails they stop what they're doing, salivate, and rush to the screen. We get the proverbial nervous tic after neglecting our e-mail for 12 hours.

This technology-enabled productivity press has led to a number of challenges. I often ask groups how many of them have been busted–meaning they have been on the phone with someone they cared about deeply and have been heard typing in the background. I know I have been on both ends of that exchange; I've felt the guilt of doing it and the personal pangs of diminishment at hearing the keyboard taps in the background. This violation is exacerbated all the more by people taking cell phone calls in friend's homes, moving cars, neighborhood stores, local theatres, and even public restrooms. And holding an office conversation with one person glued to the monitor or facilitating a meeting as participants type out e-mail has actually become acceptable in some circles. For the wired elite: always on, always connected. But are we connecting?

In his books *Connnect* and *Human Moments*, Edward Hallowell, a senior lecturer with Harvard Medical School and the Director of the Hallowell Center for Cognitive and Emotional Health in Concord (MA), talks about the irony of how many electronic connections we have today, yet how hard it is for us to form authentic and deep personal connections with our family members and friends (Hallowell, 2001). In his therapy practice he sees severe dysfunction from this lack of connection–people in real pain because they feel their relationship span is "a mile wide and an inch deep." In *The Lexus and the Olive Tree*, Thomas Friedman builds on this point by noting that many Americans are more connected to national and global communities–through constant watching of CNN, MSNBC, and other news channels–than they are to issues and people in their own cities or neighborhoods (Friedman, 2000).

Is the press to move faster and to look globally as opposed to locally going to change any time soon? I doubt it. The question is, then, can we develop the ability to be mindful of those around us in our connected fast-paced surroundings? To successfully navigate the road ahead, we must. The at-risk student, the eager learner, the colleague in need all require our focus if our work is to make a difference. To paraphrase Ghandi's admonition, we must give the gift of being truly present with those around us if we wish to make a difference. However, in the broad analysis, we have to give ourselves some slack before we berate ourselves too harshly. This *is* the fastest adoption of a disruptive technology in human history. It's not surprising that we're only beginning to develop personal and cultural norms to manage the challenges. But we cannot fail to strive to meet the need to make real connections with each other and our students, particularly with the organizational and societal road hazards in our path.

Organizational Road Hazards

One of the most common organizational road hazards has little to do with technology itself; it has to do with technology's relation to change. The hazard is the cultural challenge of *not engaging the reasoned center of the institution in meaningful explorations of the good and bad aspects of technology in education and society.* Many college conversations on technology are dominated–as are conversations on a range of other topics–by two extreme groups. One group is of caustic cynics committed to thwarting any change initiative. Sometimes caustic cynics are once-engaged professionals who have been too often burned by strategic plan after strategic plan. Based on their experience, the best course of action is inaction. From student-centered education to writing across the curriculum to MBO to TQM, they can count the fads that have washed ashore, full of presidential sound and fury, but in the end they returned nothing to the adventurous educators and students who rode the wave. Others are wrestling with personal issues far beyond the reach of rational college-based dialogue. Their arguments are often loud and logical; but scratch the surface and the seeds of fear, pain, and trauma that have little to do with the college or any specific initiative sprout to life. While these are not the only profiles that fall into this group, they both share one of the defining characteristics of caustic cynics: an almost pathological aversion to believing.

The only group that can equal in energy the venom and vigor brought to the fore by caustic cynics as they rage against the new and novel are the true believers. These professionals got religion on a given topic and cannot understand why their truth is not universally accepted by all. They extol the virtue of their tools, techniques, or paradigms and counter any criticism by labeling it as related to a personal fault in the person who dares to raise a question. They make bold claims that deserve detailed exploration, but are deeply uncomfortable with devil's advocates who question ridiculous bromides like "technology will transform education." True believers also fit multiple profiles, from good-hearted, inexperienced change agents to easily enamored zealots. And they share one of the defining characteristics of true believers: an almost pathological passion for believing.

But as Eric Hoffer, my favorite longshoreman philosopher, put so well:

> *In times of drastic change, it is the learners who inherit the future. The learned usually find themselves equipped to live in a world that no longer exists.*

It is in the cool, reasoned center, swimming with thoughtful critics and reasoned advocates, where learners can soak in the best ways to use technology and discover the keys to not being used *by* technology. Yet in many institutions, the learned loud voices of the extremes frighten the best of faculty and staff away. Talented and caring educators determine that it's not wise to invest energy and effort in dialectic dialogues dominated by dogmatic diatribes. *Hunker down and do your job* becomes the modus operandi. It's sad. Moreover, it's paralyzing for institutions in dire need of real conversation about how to help students learn about, with, and beyond technology.

When educators in the reasoned center rise up, however, good things can happen–especially if they respect the rights of the extremes to hold their opinions, but refuse to allow them to control the destiny of the institution. It's never easy; and it usually requires significant individual courage coupled with top administration and faculty leadership. However, by navigating through this road hazard, the journey for the institution is much more energizing. Moreover, we model the best of inclusive and yeasty participation in organizational life for our students.

Another common organizational cultural road hazard is *the search for simple answers to complex questions about technology*. For example, one of the most frequent straw-man arguments advanced whenever technology and learning comes up is the famous *Which is better, online learning or in-class learning?* While it may seem an appealing contrast, it is rife with complexities that make the results of the best-designed studies almost meaningless.

All of us have worked our way through education systems and can name teachers who have changed our lives–or at least lit a fire of interest on a given topic–and others we would not wish on our worst enemy. In addition, there are teaching techniques that, applied well, engage students in powerful ways. For example collaborative learning can break through learning logjams in fields from biology to philosophy. That said, all of us can point to an experience of being in a small group exercise that was excruciatingly useless. Finally, some students have *no* choice about their mode of instruction. Life situation, time constraints, and learning style often dictate the way in which learning will be received. Are we really willing to shut the door to learning to anyone who is unwilling to learn as *we* did?

Whether it's in class or on line, quality is more likely related to who is involved in instruction (teachers and learners), the quality of the curriculum, the multiple modes of delivery, and the learning strategies engaged. Indeed, as Web learning emerged in 1996, then League for Innovation President Terry O'Banion made the point that while great things might be ahead, we needed to confront the reality that the Web "holds the horrible potential of making already terrible instruction that much more available." Moreover, with the ever-more-common hybrid models of delivery–including elements of in-class and online tools across classes and programs–the comparison of modes becomes even more problematic. Finally, an admonition worth noting here comes from a theme that wove its way through every stage of the *Practical Magic* study on teaching-excellence-award winners. Faculty in this study warned again and again to beware of anyone claiming to know the final answer: *the experience of these educators show there clearly is not one best way to teach!*

Yet another quest for simple answers to complex questions surrounds technology ROI: Return on Investment. As the dotcom bubble burst and businesses again accepted the longstanding importance of a little thing called profit, so too did they begin to look at their technology purchases and work to relate them directly to their bottom lines. Complex metrics that capture multiple value principles emerged, such as applied information economics, customer index, balanced scorecard, economic value added, economic value sourced, and real option valuation, and have become essential parts of technology reviews.

The debate about ROI in industry is mirrored by the conflict over the creation of concrete ROI measures in education. We have a complex combination of fiscal, operational, service, and learning variables to consider with regard to technology. Does IT help us improve our bottom lines, smooth operations, expand student service, and– the Holy Grail–improve learning? The importance of these variable sets is fiercely debated as any ROI discussion emerges, a debate made even more challenging by the distinction between cognitive and discrete skill measures of learning. Moreover, there is a cost-of-entry issue regarding technology in education. Without a certain level of technology services and learning options, many students will not consider attending your institution as we boldly move into the 21st century. In the business world, it's called the pay-to-play principle.

In the end, whether it's looking for the best way to teach or not teach with IT or exploring ROI for technology in our colleges or wrestling with the ever-popular techno-against-humanist, high-tech versus high-touch debate, we have to be willing to search for answers without jumping to simple or predisposed views. These are meaty issues not easily resolved. The answers almost always include a caveat: it depends. Therein is the major hazard. Just as we must encourage organizational conversations with an acceptance of diverse opinions, we must be comfortable with complexity in answers when we pose complex questions. Ironically, small- and large-scale IT initiatives can be stalled for months or years because of this phenomenon. Many times we are too eager to find one best way or an incontrovertible answer before we decide. This clinging to the desire for simple answers makes us eminently less able to steer clear of organizational road hazards.

The final hazard I'll mention in this section is actually inclusive of both the individual and organizational level. *All too often because of fear, ignorance, or exhaustion, individuals and organizations relinquish control and let information technology happen to them.* Recently I was a part of a conversation in which a highly intelligent educational professional proudly pronounced his refusal to get a cell phone. He said, "I just don't want to be answering a phone all the time, to be at the mercy of people's expectations." A caring colleague, also in the conversation, gently noted that unreasonable expectations are indeed frustrating, but that this weakness in others had not stopped her from taking the cell phone plunge. She noted, "I just had to learn that these little things have an off button. I only use it when *I* want to. And now I just love the convenience." I wish I could have taken a picture of the proud pronouncer's face as he contemplated her response. It was as though he'd never realized you could turn cell phones *off.*

I had a similar epiphany when a good friend made the observation that turning off the feature in my e-mail program that automatically checks for new messages is the ultimate cure for the Pavlovian e-mail syndrome. When retrieving new messages must be triggered manually, you suddenly gain control of when and why your messages flood into the inbox. This little change has made all the difference in the world–particularly as I do things like write this chapter. In the past, if I had my e-mail program on in the background, the tempting little sound that welcomed new messages would constantly draw me to check for office emergencies. I've taken it one step further: I've begun turning off my monitor or closing my laptop lid whenever I'm at my desk but not using the computer.

A more concrete teaching and learning example confronts me whenever I speak at a college or event. Very often, because I use technology as an element in my presentations, a technology support person is put in charge of my speaker setup. Often these professionals are incredibly accommodating; some call months in advance to prepare the setting to any specifications I desire. I love these folks. With my presentation and workshop style, their willingness to adapt makes all the difference in the world. Because I enjoy connecting with the participants in an effort to create greater energy in the room, I prefer no lecterns, a wireless lapel microphone, and a small, discreet table for my laptop placed close to the audience. I want to be able to literally reach out and touch the folks with whom I'm working. This setup just changes the dynamic, especially when we're exploring challenging topics like technology in education or strategies for reaching at-risk students.

Sometimes, though, it's impossible to make an early connection with anyone in charge of the setting. Or, because we are part of a larger program, the room has been preset by the hotel or by a theater tech-support team. The corresponding awkward situations–for example being placed at the back of a deep stage behind a tall lectern facing a theater too large for the group with an angry audience sitting in the back rows struggling to see projected PowerPoint in a fully darkened room–have taught me to arrive very early to any speaking engagement. I try to be as gracious as possible, but I have learned that for the sake of the audience, I have to take as much *control* as possible of the learning situation and manipulate the environment. Of course, any good teacher does this on entering a classroom. I have literally marched my laptop and RGB video cable out to the middle of a theater or multipurpose room to join the faculty and staff in dialogue. But sometimes these moves challenge and threaten tech-support or logistics persons, so much so that they rebel. Sometimes they lie. I have been told with a straight face by technical people that something I knew was possible was *impossible* and that I'd have to do it their way. It suddenly becomes a control issue.

It's clear to me that some educators are at the mercy of those willing to take control of technology. They suffer in classrooms and on software systems that are not designed to meet their needs or the needs of their students. Often because we don't know what is possible or even what questions to ask, *we end up feeling like we are no longer using technology, but are being used by it.* From annoying classroom technology configurations to multimillion-dollar ERP system choices, some essential decisions that impact the entire college community are turned over to individuals who care little about teaching or reaching students. Alan Cooper is the father of the Virtual Basic programming language and a true technology insider who wrote the book *The Inmates Are Running the Asylum: Why High Tech Products Drive Us Crazy and How To Restore the Sanity* (1999). In it, he observes that through no ill will or evil intent, crucial decisions in business are being driven by technologists designing software and hardware. For the most part, these professionals love technology, which is why the quest for innovative features and functions propels increasingly complex and ultimately less useful technology. He argues that if businesses are to gain better control of their journeys on the road ahead, there will have to be an emphasis on developing either more technology-savvy businesspeople or more business-savvy technologists. Of course, the corollary for education is equally true; as we move along the road ahead, we can gain greater control of our learning environments by fostering and supporting the development of more technology-savvy educators and more education-savvy technologists.

This need for a sort of technology renaissance leader has made the quest for the ideal chief technology officer or chief information officer in education problematic. Do you look for someone who knows the education world, with its academic freedom, participatory decision processes, and student-centered focus, and hope that person can develop or hire subordinates with good technology skills? Or do you seek out the best technologist possible, allowing for the time it will take to learn the academic culture? As you have probably already guessed, the answer is most likely, *It depends.*

Whoever we hire, we have to make a choice. And our perspective toward these choices with regard to technology is what really counts; we have to own them and ground them in some construct or purpose. For example, colleges in the League for Innovation Learning College Project have adopted learning-centered education as their guide to technology choices (http://www.league.org/league/projects/lcp/). Any technology tool or technique has to prove that it will ultimately improve or expand learning. While this perspective seems simplistic, when these issues are explored with honest and tough-minded debate, ever more meaningful technology choices emerge. The alternative is to turn these decisions over to someone and spread the blame. However, as the proponents of internal locus of control expound (Flowers, 1994), if we choose this path and play the victim on either the individual or organizational level, we will be hard pressed to handle the stress of preparing students for an increasingly complex, connected world–a world filled with sometimes frightening societal hazards.

Societal Road Hazards

Even with the loss of more than seven trillion dollars in market capital since the dotcom crash, it is still easy to become wrapped up in the optimism and excitement that can surround technology discussions. Indeed, I am more often than not eagerly looking ahead to the world my children will experience. As natives in a digital technology world, their experiences and perspectives will be strikingly different from my own techno-immigrant viewpoint. Someday I'll be forced to confess to them that I thought Pong was an exciting video game, and that in my grade school, a rolling slide show accompanied by cassette-tape narration was a high-tech multimedia event. Not so for them. They will never know a world without computer-generated animation, Internet, e-mail, or sophisticated search engines that put information from sources across the globe at their fingertips. But they will also be challenged to avoid hazards in their youth the likes of which no generation has ever faced.

At a conference last year, I was struck by the story of an 11-year-old boy who was at the center of a horrific child-abuse case. Earlier that month, he had chosen for a class project the topic of celebrity impersonators. He immediately jumped on the Internet and put "celebrity impersonators" in a search engine, and up came thousands of links. The first few were interesting. But then, quite by accident, he clicked on a hyperlink that launched him into a pornography site that seized his computer. Suddenly, pop-up window after pop-up window came onto the screen. The faster he closed them, the faster they appeared. He finally decided to turn off the computer in hopes of wiping the Web intruder off his desktop, but little did he know that somewhere in all the clicking and popping, the intrusive site had changed the default home page on the computer's Internet Browser to a pornography site. Later that day, his father came home, launched the browser and was also swept away in a flashflood of pop-up pornography. In his surprise and anger, the father leaped to the conclusion that his son had been cruising these sites, and he proceeded to beat the boy until he was bloody and bruised.

This example is equaled in its chilling effect only by last year's break in the Operation Candyman child pornography sting. In a March 2002 story in The *New York Times*, David Stout reports:

> A nationwide Internet child-pornography ring has been smashed with the arrest of about 90 people, including two Roman Catholic priests, a school bus driver, a teacher's aide and a police officer, federal authorities said today.
>
> "It is clear that a new marketplace for child pornography has emerged from the dark corners of cyberspace," Attorney General John Ashcroft said at a news briefing. "Innocent boys and girls have been targeted by offenders who view them as sexual objects.". . .
>
> One Web site advertised itself as "for people who love kids," the authorities said. The site invited people to "post any type of messages you like" and offered a postscript: "If we all work together, we will have the best group on the Net."[†]

For the last seven years, commerce on legal adult pornography sites was the biggest moneymaker on the Net, grossing billions as the industry expanded operations on and offshore. Now, online gambling has eclipsed pornography as the largest moneymaker, and it is poised to become a global powerhouse (http://www.msnbc.com/news/544764.asp). As you

[†]Copyright © 2002 by the New York Times Co. Reprinted by permission.

likely know, both the online gambling and pornography industries invest millions in highly sophisticated technology and aggressive *sticky-marketing* strategies–techniques that aim to suck surfers in, capturing their attention, loyalty, and dollars (http://www.sticky-marketing.net/).

These are the same techniques adopted by hate groups over the last decade. If you visit Tolerance.org, a website sponsored by the Southern Poverty Law Center, you can learn more about how hate groups have grown to love the Internet, leveraging its associated tools to organize and spread their venom locally, nationally, and internationally. You can literally track hate groups across the United States (http://www.tolerance.org/maps/hate/) and see graphic examples of their sticky Web strategies in action (http://www.tolerance.org/hate_internet/). And for a final look at the face of evil online, explore the use of the Internet by international terrorists to raise money, coordinate attacks, and recruit new followers (see *Newsweek's* October 2001 story, "The Road to September 11"). It's clear from the reports of law enforcement agencies from the FBI (http://www.fbi.gov/) to Interpol (http://www.interpol.int/) that international terrorists have aggressively adopted and leveraged what many in the United States see as the ultimate symbol of intellectual freedom and exchange: the Internet.

But lest we think it's just the extremes that should concern us, *let's not forget the powerful tools at the fingertips of all business, government, religious, and political organizations.* Each of these sectors is urged to develop strong Customer Relationship Management (CRM) systems that track as many of our interactions as possible. Indeed, most credit card companies today employ sophisticated artificial intelligence engines capable of almost 95 percent accuracy in detecting when your card is stolen. No, they don't have cameras nationwide–that's the purview of the U.S. National Security Agency (NSA) and, soon, the office of Homeland Security. What the credit-card companies have is your shopping profile. If something is bought that does not fit within your standard predicted profile, the system automatically alerts the fraud department, which immediately tasks a service agent to contact you.

I was made aware of these systems a little over two years ago, after I received a cell-phone call from my credit card company asking if I had lost my card. I didn't know it was lost; it must have fallen out of my PDA case only 30 minutes earlier at a local coffeehouse. I thought to myself: this major multinational company with thousands of employees and billions in assets has a system to detect irregularities in my buying behavior that is so sophisticated that it can spot possible theft of my credit card and contact me all in a 30-minute period! While I was thankful for the service, the incident did give me pause.

Churches are also beginning to expand their reach online. Major Christian denominations all have extensive websites and are piloting a range of worship services and fundraising techniques (e.g., www.baptist.org, www.unitedmethodist.org, www.presbyterianchurch.org, www.catholic.org), as are Muslims (e.g., www.muslim.org, www.islam.org), Buddhists (e.g., www.dharmanet.org, www.prajnaparamita.com), Hindus (e.g., www.hindu.org, www.hindunet.org), and Taoists (e.g., www.taoist.org, www.tao.org).

In addition to businesses and churches, on the political front we are girding for the 2004 Presidential Election, which will arguably be the most Web-focused election yet. Campaign managers are already designing detailed sites, to connect with potential voters and spread their messages far and wide. From President George Bush (http://www.whitehouse.gov/) to his potential rivals John Kerry (http://www.johnkerry.com/), Joe Lieberman (http://www.joe2004.com), and John Edwards (http://www.johnedwards2004.com/), the online race has already begun. And if businesses and governments can use artificial-intelligence engines to predict our shopping behavior or civic loyalty, how long do you think it will be before the major political parties have a comprehensive CRM system of their own to drive affiliation and fundraising? You don't need to wait at all; it's already here (http://www.politicsonline.com). A Digital Democracy indeed!

Turning Toward DotCalm

In a 2001 *Educause Review* article titled "Education in a Digital Democracy," Cindy Miles and I noted the Jefforsonian challenge of our time. As the champion of public education in the United States, Jefferson saw education's broadest purpose as providing the foundation for freedom and democracy. He made the bold claim that "if a society expects to be ignorant and free, it wants what never was and what never will be." This statement has never been truer than it is today; so many have information at their fingertips, yet are not sure what to do with it. Thomas Friedman makes the point well:

> At its best, the Internet can educate more people faster than any media tool we've ever had. At its worst, it can make people dumber faster than any media tool we've ever had. The lie that 4,000 Jews were warned not to go into the World Trade Center on September 11 was spread entirely over the Internet and is now thoroughly believed in the Muslim world. Because the Internet has an aura of "technology" surrounding it, the uneducated believe information from it even more. They don't realize that the Internet, at its ugliest, is just an open sewer: an electronic conduit for untreated, unfiltered information.
>
> –Thomas Friedman, The New York Times, 2002

The implications of our choices with and uses of information are profound. These choices will dictate whether or not we and our students can truly live free in this increasingly connected world. Indeed, no amount of slowing down will help if we don't recognize the individual, organizational, and societal hazards, or if we aren't wise enough to understand why they're hazardous!

Therefore, as engaged educators we must continue to champion the liberal-arts underpinnings of education–communication; computation; critical thinking; problem solving; information management; interpersonal, personal, and community skills–even as we strive to include broader segments of society in the Information Age. We must strive to give our students the ability to learn, earn, and live well, and to participate as active citizens in a vibrant, connected community.

Michael Novak is the George Federick Jewett Chair in Religion and Public Policy at the American Enterprise Institute for Public Policy and Research, and the author of several books on life in a democracy. Speaking at a recent meeting of the Business Higher Education Forum, Novak noted the importance of today's educational institutions' emphasizing core habits. He argued that there are core habits necessary for a democracy and a market economy to work, habits such as creativity and innovation, enterprise and effort, community involvement and care, and realism and accountability. To this list I would add courage. The courage to thoughtfully move down the road ahead, hazards and all, ever filled with the expectations of creating a better person, a better organization, and a better world.

We've gone careening down the road to DotCom and we know now where that leads. There has to be a better way. Maybe it's time to slow down, look around, and get on the road to DotCalm, a place where we can thoughtfully engage and explore all aspects of technology–good, bad, or indifferent; a place where we can move beyond love affairs with the new and novel to a passion for the essential and important; a place beyond frantic multitasking to a mindful focus on the people and passions that make life worth living.

And let's bring as many along with us as we can.

REFERENCES

Christensen, C. (1997). *The Innovator's Dilemma*. Cambridge, MA: Harvard Business School Press.

Friedman, T. (2002). Global Village Idiocy and the Community College. In League for Innovation in the Community College *Leadership Abstracts*, *15*(6). Available: www.league.org/publication/abstracts/leadership/labs0602.html.

Greenspan, A. (2002, October). Productivity. In Federal Reserve Board Speach, *U.S. Department of Labor and American Enterprise Institute Conference*, Washington, DC. Avaliable: www.federalreserve.gov/boarddocs/speeches/2002/20021023/default.htm.

Hallowell, E. (1999). *Connect*. New York: Pantheon.

Hallowell, E. (2001). *Human Moments*. New York: Health Communications.

McGrath, M. (2000). *Product Strategy for High Technology Companies*. New York: McGraw-Hill.

Newell, F., & Rogers, M. (2000). *loyalty.com*: *Customer Relationship Management in the New Era of Internet Marketing*. New York: McGraw-Hill.

Milliron, M., & Miles, C. (1998). The Technology Prayers. In From the Facilitator, League for Innovation in the Community College *Technology and Learning Community* (TLC). Available: www.leaguetlc.org.

Milliron, M., & Miles, C. (1998, April 22). Simple Prayers for the Blessings–and the Curses–of Technology. *Community College Week*.

Milliron, M., & Miles, C. (2001). Education in a Digital Democracy. *Educause Review*. Available: www.educause.edu/pub/er/erm00/articles006/erm0064.pdf.

Milliron, M. (2002). Getting a Kick out of Learning. *Converge Magazine.* Available: www.convergemag.com/magazine/story.phtml?id=38206.

Novak, M. (2003, February). *Winter Business Higher Education Forum,* LaJolla, CA.

Novak, M. (1982). *The Spirit of Democratic Capitalism.* New York: Simon & Schuster.

Stout, D. (2002, March 19). Candyman Sting. *The New York Times.*

AMADO M. PEÑA, JR.

I feel blessed having seen and touched the beautiful things that speak so proudly of who we are. Our gifts to the world are our history and our art.

– Amado M. Peña, Jr.

Canyon de Chelley, Monument Valley, Spider Rock, Enchanted Mesa, Acoma, Black Mesa–these are names that evoke an aura of mystery and hint at the birth of legends. These sites are part of an enduring, rugged landscape that speaks of the ancient heritage of a region now known as Arizona and New Mexico. This land, the people who live there, and their native crafts, are the threads in a rich cultural tapestry that is the inspiration for the works of Amado M. Peña, Jr. Using this trilogy of imagery, Peña studies the interrelation and integration of these entities, giving each equal importance. Peña, a mestizo of Mexican and Yaqui ancestry, celebrates the strength of a people who meet the harsh realities of life in an uncompromising land, and his work is a tribute to these Native Americans who survive by living in harmony with an adversarial, untamed environment.

Using bold color, form, and the dynamics of composition, Peña communicates his vision of a land, a people, and their art. He is a prolific artist with restless creative energy that keeps him at work in his studios in Santa Fe, New Mexico, and Austin, Texas. A master printer, his serigraphs are noted for bold color schemes and strong graphic use of lines. His etchings convey quiet elegance in fine lines and soft color. The drama of his paintings is heightened by an intensity of hue and unexpected spatial relationships. Abstractions of the landscape merge with exaggerated human forms; blanket and pottery patterns further echo the shapes of the land.

Although his admirers come from different cultures and traditions, from all ages and parts of the world, the strength of his vision crosses such boundaries and speaks to them of hope, endurance, and the unconquerable dignity of man. These qualities are etched into the faces of Amado M. Peña, Jr.'s art.

Peña Studio Gallery, the exclusive representative of Amado M. Peña, Jr., exhibits a full range of his original paintings, drawing, graphics, ceramics, and wearables. For further information, please contact Peña Studio Gallery in Santa Fe, New Mexico.

www.penagallery.com
1-888-220-PENA
penagallery@earthlink.net

THE LEAGUE'S DIGITAL DIVIDE PROJECT

The technological advances of the Digital Age provide unparalleled access to information. However, these advances have led to what many have called the Digital Divide, where technological opportunities are disproportionately distant from minority and economically challenged populations. Community college educators must take an aggressive stance in finding quality ways to teach and reach our diverse student cohorts and communities. The Bridging the Digital Divide Project provides collaborative opportunities for community college educators, community leaders, and corporate partners to work together to better define this complex issue and build effective bridges to lessen the gap between the information haves and have-nots.

The purpose of the Bridging the Digital Divide Project is to inspire community college educators to take the strategic and aggressive steps to help provide the necessary information technology access and skill sets for a growing number of minorities and economically challenged populations.

During the 2000 *Conference on Information Technology* (CIT) in Anaheim, California, the League hosted the Digital Divide Summit in which Digital Divide leaders highlighted model programs and current trends and facilitated interactive focus groups aimed at helping the League define broadscale Digital Divide projects. Speakers included George Boggs, President, American Association of Community Colleges; Norman Fortenberry, Director, Division of Undergraduate Education, National Science Foundation; and David Bolt, Executive Producer, PBS Digital Divide Series, Studio Miramar. As part of existing contributions and commitment to helping address the complex challenges surrounding the Digital Divide, the League published *Access in the Information Age: Community Colleges Bridging the Digital Divide*. This book, *From Digital Divide to Digital Democracy*, is the second in the series. While the first publication focuses on broad, institutionwide recommendations and approaches to bridging the Digital Divide, the second focuses on Digital Divide issues that community college educators, business partners, and community agency leaders collaboratively help to define through further League-coordinated focus groups, surveys, and information sharing.

The research findings, recommendations, model programs, and successful strategies described in this book should provide useful background or stimulus for more complete conversations and explorations that we hope have started or will emerge soon in all academic communities. By moving beyond definition and dialogue to strategic action, community colleges are well positioned to lead the way toward a Digital Democracy.